Contents

I0105332

Published by Michigan Legal Publishing Ltd.
Grand Rapids, Michigan

Academic and bulk discounts available at
www.michlp.com

Lesson 1: Course Overview

Visual 1:   Course Welcome

The Emergency Management Institute developed the IS-200.c Basic Incident Command System for Initial Response, ICS 200 course in collaboration with:

- National Wildfire Coordinating Group (NWCG)
- U.S. Department of Agriculture (USDA)
- U.S. Fire Administration's National Fire Programs Branch
- United States Coast Guard (USCG)

IS-200.c follows NIMS guidelines and meets the National Incident Management System (NIMS) Baseline Training requirements for ICS 200.

Note	This course is a part of the series of ICS courses designed to meet the all-hazards, all-agency NIMS ICS requirement for operational personnel. Descriptions and details about the other ICS courses in the series may be found on our Web site: http://training.fema.gov.

Visual 2:   Course Objectives

This course is designed to enable personnel to operate efficiently during an incident or event within the Incident Command System (ICS) and focuses on the management of an initial response to an incident.

Overall Course Objectives

At the end of the course, you should be able to:

- Describe the course objectives and summarize basic information about the Incident Command System (ICS) and National Incident Management System (NIMS).
- Describe how the NIMS Management Characteristics relate to Incident Command and Unified Command.
- Describe the delegation of authority process, implementing authorities, management by objectives, and preparedness plans and objectives.
- Identify ICS organizational components, the Command Staff, the General Staff, and ICS tools.
- Describe different types of briefings and meetings.
- Explain flexibility within the standard ICS organizational structure.
- Explain transfer of command briefings and procedures.
- Use ICS to manage an incident or event.

Visual 3:   Student Introductions

Introduce yourself by providing:

- Your name
- Your job title
- A brief statement of your overall experience with emergency or incident response
- Your possible roles in responding to incidents

Visual 4:   Student Expectations

?

What do you expect to gain from this course?

Visual 5:   Instructor Expectations

- Cooperate with the group.
- Be open minded to new ideas.
- Participate actively in all of the training activities.
- Return to class at the stated time.
- Use what you learn in the course to perform effectively within an ICS organization.

Visual 6:   Course Structure

This course is divided into eight units plus the Course Summary.

- Unit 1: Course Overview
- Unit 2: Incident Command and Unified Command
- Unit 3: Delegation of Authority and Management by Objectives
- Unit 4: Functional Areas and Positions
- Unit 5: Incident Briefings and Meetings
- Unit 6: Organizational Flexibility
- Unit 7: Transfer of Command
- Unit 8: Application Activity
- Unit 9: Course Summary

Visual 7:   Course Logistics

Review the following information:

- Course agenda
- Sign-in sheet
- Breaks
- Message and telephone location
- Cell phone policy
- Facilities
- Other concerns

Visual 8:   Agenda

DAY 1	DAY 2
Morning Session	Morning Session
• Unit 1: Course Overview • Unit 2: Incident Command and Unified Command	Unit 6: Organizational Flexibility
Afternoon Session	Afternoon Session
• Unit 3: Delegation of Authority & Management by Objectives • Unit 4: Functional Areas & Positions	• Unit 7: Transfer of Command • Unit 8: Application Activity • Unit 9: Course Summary and Final Exam

Visual 9:   Course Completion

In order to successfully complete this course, you must:

- Participate in unit activities.
- Achieve 75% or higher on the final exam.
- Complete the end-of-course evaluation.

Unit Objectives

This unit provides an overview of the Incident Command System (ICS) and the National Incident Management System (NIMS).

At the end of this unit, you should be able to:

- Describe the Incident Command System (ICS).
- Describe the National Incident Management System (NIMS).

Visual 10:   Lesson 1 Overview

This lesson provides an overview of the Incident Command System (ICS) and the National Incident Management System (NIMS).

Lesson Objectives

At the end of this lesson, you should be able to:

- Describe the Incident Command System (ICS).
- Describe the National Incident Management System (NIMS).

Visual 11:   Incident Command System (ICS)

ICS:

- Is a standardized management tool for meeting the demands of small or large emergency or nonemergency situations
- Represents "best practices," and has become the standard for emergency management across the country
- May be used for planned events, natural disasters, and acts of terrorism
- Is a part of the National Incident Management System (NIMS)

ICS is not just a standardized organizational chart, but an entire management system.

Visual 12:   Why ICS?

All levels of government, the private sector, and
nongovernmental agencies must be prepared to prevent, protect
against, mitigate, respond to, and recover from a wide spectrum
of major events and natural disasters that exceed the capabilities
of any single entity. Threats from natural disasters and human-
caused events, such as terrorism, require a unified and
coordinated national approach to planning and to domestic
incident management.

Visual 13:   Homeland Security Presidential Directives

HSPD-5, Management of Domestic Incidents, identified steps for improved coordination in response to incidents. It required the Department of Homeland Security (DHS) to coordinate with other Federal departments and agencies and State, local, and tribal governments to establish a National Response Framework (NRF) and a National Incident Management System (NIMS).

HSPD-8, National Preparedness, directed DHS to lead a national initiative to develop a National Preparedness System—a common, unified approach to "strengthen the preparedness of the United States to prevent and respond to threatened or actual domestic terrorist attacks, major disasters, and other emergencies."

Presidential Policy Directive 8 (PPD-8), National Preparedness, describes the Nation's approach to preparedness-one that involves the whole community, including individuals, businesses, community- and faith-based organizations, schools, tribes, and all levels of government (Federal, State, local, tribal and territorial).

Note	**HSPD-5, HSPD-8, and PPD-8** Copies of the HSPD-5, Management of Domestic Incidents, HSPD-8, National Preparedness, and Presidential Policy Directive 8 (PPD-8), National Preparedness can be found online. Please use the links below to access them. HSPD-5, Management of Domestic Incidents: https://www.dhs.gov/publication/homeland-security-presidential-directive-5 HSPD-8, National Preparedness: https://www.gpo.gov/fdsys/pkg/PPP-2003-book2/pdf/PPP-2003-book2-doc-pg1745.pdf Presidential Policy Directive 8 (PPD-8), National Preparedness: https://www.dhs.gov/presidential-policy-directive-8-national-preparedness

Visual 14: National Incident Management System (NIMS) Overview

NIMS provides a consistent framework for incident management at all jurisdictional levels regardless of the cause, size, or complexity of the incident.

NIMS provides the Nation's first responders and authorities with the same foundation for incident management for terrorist attacks, natural disasters, and other emergencies.

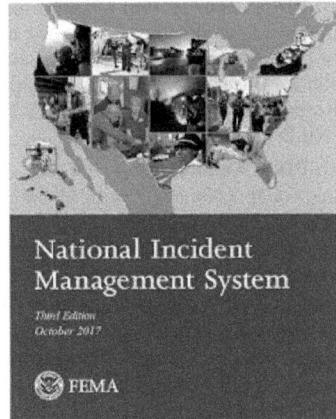

National Incident Management System

Third Edition
October 2017

FEMA

Note

Implementing NIMS

According to the National Integration Center, "Implementing the use of NIMS" means that government officials, incident managers, and emergency response organizations at all jurisdictional levels adopt the National Incident Management System. Actions to implement the use of NIMS take place at two levels - policy and organizational/operational.

At the policy level, implementing NIMS means government officials, i.e., governors, mayors, county and city managers, tribal leaders, and others:

- Adopt the NIMS through executive order, proclamation, or legislation as the jurisdiction's official incident response system; and
- Direct that incident managers and response organizations in their jurisdictions train, exercise, and use the NIMS in their response operations.

At the organizational/operational level, evidence that incident managers and emergency response organizations are implementing NIMS would include the following:

- NIMS is being integrated into functional and system-wide emergency operations policies, plans, and procedures.
- NIMS training is planned or under way for responders, supervisors, and command level officers; and
- Incident personnel at all levels are participating and/or coordinating exercises involving NIMS structures and responders from multiple

---

disciplines and jurisdictions.

The NIMS doctrine can be found at: www.fema.gov/national-incident-management-system

Visual 15:   Major Components of NIMS

Jurisdictions and organizations involved in the management of incidents vary in their authorities, management structures, communication capabilities and protocols, and many other factors.

The major components of NIMS provide a common framework to integrate these diverse capabilities and achieve common goals.

The application of all three components is vital to successful NIMS implementation.

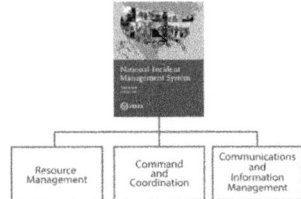

Note	Resource Management
	Resource Management describes standard mechanisms to systematically manage resources, including personnel, equipment, supplies, teams, and facilities, both before and during incidents in order to allow organizations to more effectively share resources when needed.

Note	Command and Coordination
	Command and Coordination describes leadership roles, processes, and recommended organizational structures for incident management at the operational and incident support levels and explains how these structures interact to manage incidents effectively and efficiently.

Note	Communications and Information Management
	Communications and Information Management describes systems and methods that help to ensure that incident personnel and other decision makers have the means and information they need to make and communicate decisions.

Visual 16:   NIMS Management Characteristics: Overview

	NIMS Management Characteristics
	The following video will introduce the NIMS Management Characteristics discussed in detail in this unit.
Video	Video Duration: 2 minutes, 30 seconds

NIMS Management Characteristics: Overview

Video Transcript

As you learned in the previous lesson, ICS is based on proven NIMS management principles, which contribute to the strength and efficiency of the overall system.

ICS incorporates a wide range of management features and principles, beginning with the use of common terminology.

[David Burns, Emergency Preparedness Manager, University of California Los Angeles] Communication is probably one of the most essential elements of ICS. It's important that we know how to communicate.

[Daryl Lee Spiewak, Former Emergency Programs Manager, the Brazos River Authority] If the terms that I use mean different things to different people, we're going to have a hard time communicating and doing what needs to be done to accomplish our mission.

ICS emphasizes effective planning, including management by objectives and reliance on an Incident Action Plan.

[Roberta Runge, EPA National NIMS Coordinator] You have to coordinate on what your end objective is. All up and down the chain you have to have a common end goal. So you can establish your objectives, you can ensure they're in the Incident Action Plan, and you can ensure that they are in agreement.

ICS employs a modular organizational structure that can be tailored based on the size, complexity and hazards of an incident. Command of this organization is established under a single Incident Commander or a Unified Command.

The ICS features related to command structure include chain of command and unity of command.

[Bill Campbell, Former Director of Training, New York State Emergency Management Office] One of the benefits is it gets all of the different organizations working under the same framework.

ICS helps ensure full utilization of all incident resources by:

- Maintaining a manageable span of control
- Establishing designated incident facilities and locations
- Implementing comprehensive resource management practices
- Defining clear processes for dispatch/ deployment of resources
- Ensuring integrated communications

ICS supports responders and decision makers through effective information and intelligence management.

[Kristy Plourde, Emergency Management Specialist, U.S. Coast Guard] The common operating picture is a critical thing that the Coast Guard has been working hard on recently for ourselves because it's something that helps us maintain a better operational picture and it's more consistent across the board, everyone up and down the chain of command and across to other agencies understand the same picture.

ICS counts on each of us taking personal accountability for our own actions. And finally, the mobilization process helps ensure that incident objectives can be achieved while responders remain safe.

[Kristy Plourde, Emergency Management Specialist, U.S. Coast Guard] To have NIMS work effectively, it's got to be top-down support.

The NIMS Management Characteristics covered in this lesson form the basis for effective, team-based incident response under the Incident Command System (ICS).

Visual 17:   NIMS Management Characteristics: Overview

This course builds on what you learned in ICS 100 about NIMS Management Characteristics. The NIMS Management Characteristics are listed below.

- Common Terminology
- Modular Organization
- Management by Objectives
- Incident Action Planning
- Manageable Span of Control
- Incident Facilities and Locations
- Comprehensive Resource Management

- Integrated Communications
- Establishment and Transfer of Command
- Unified Command
- Chain of Command and Unity of Command
- Accountability
- Dispatch/Deployment
- Information and Intelligence Management

Visual 18:   NIMS Management Characteristics: Activity 1.1

Activity Purpose: To see how much you remember from ICS-100 about NIMS Management Characteristics.

Time: 35 minutes

Instructions:

- Divide into table teams.
- Instructions:
    - Your team will have 3 minutes to try to list as many NIMS Management Characteristics as you can remember. Hint: There are 14 features.
    - Select a spokesperson and recorder.
    - Start writing when the Instructor says "go."
    - Stop when the Instructor calls time.
- Post your team's list.

NIMS Management Characteristics: Activity 1.1 Review

Activity Purpose: To see how much you remember from ICS-100 about NIMS Management Characteristics.

Time: 35 minutes

Instructions:

Activity

- Divide into table teams.
- Instructions:
    - Your team will have 3 minutes to try to list as many NIMS Management Characteristics as you can remember. Hint: There are 14 features.
    - Select a spokesperson and recorder.
    - Start writing when the Instructor says "go."
    - Stop when the Instructor calls time.
- Post your team's list.

NIMS Management Characteristics - Supplemental Materials

NIMS Management Characteristic: Common Terminology

NIMS establishes common terminology that allows different organizations to work together in a wide variety of emergency functions and hazard scenarios.

Common terminology helps by reducing confusion and enhancing interoperability.

This common terminology covers:

- **Organizational Functions**: Major functions and units are named and defined using standardized terms
- **Resource Descriptions**: Resources (personnel, equipment, teams and facilities) have common naming based on their type and capabilities
- **Incident Facilities**: Facilities in an incident area are designated using common terms

NIMS Management Characteristic: Modular Organization

Organizational structures for incident management (ICS and EOCs) are modular, meaning that they are each building blocks that are put in place as needed based on an incident's size, complexity and hazards.

The ICS Commander and EOC director are responsible for the establishment and expansion of the modular organization based on the specific requirements for their incident.

As incident complexity increases, the organizational structure expands and management responsibilities are further divided.

The number of management, supervisory, and support positions expand as needed to meet the needs of the incident.

NIMS Management Characteristic: Management by Objectives

In an incident, all activities are directed to accomplish defined objectives. This is called Management by Objectives.

Under ICS the Incident Commander (or Unified Command) establishes incident objectives.

Management by objectives includes:

- Establishing specific, measurable objectives
- Identifying strategies, tactics, tasks, and activities to achieve the objectives
- Developing and issuing assignments, plans, procedures and protocols to accomplish tasks
- Documenting results against objectives to measure performance, facilitate corrective actions, and inform development of objectives for the next operational period

NIMS Management Characteristic: Incident Action Planning

Incident action planning guides incident management activities.

Action Plans:

- Record and communicate incident objectives, tactics, and assignments for operations and support
- Are recommended for all incidents
- Are not always written, but a written IAP is increasingly important when an incident or activation:
  - Is likely to extend beyond one operational period
  - Becomes more complex
  - Involves multiple jurisdictions or agencies

NIMS Management Characteristic: Manageable Span of Control

Span of control refers to the number of subordinates that directly report to a supervisor.

Maintaining an appropriate span of control ensures effective incident management by enabling supervisors to:

- Direct and supervise subordinates
- Communicate with and manage resources

The optimal span of control for incident management is one supervisor to five subordinates; however, the 1:5 ratio is only a guideline and effective incident management often calls for different ratios.

When a supervisor's span of control becomes unmanageable, they can assign subordinate supervisors or redistribute subordinates to manage portions of the organization in order to regain a manageable span of control.

Span of control can change based on:

- Type of incident
- Nature of the task
- Existing hazards and safety factors
- Distances between personnel and resources

NIMS Management Characteristic: Incident Facilities and Locations

The Incident Commander, Unified Command or EOC director establishes incident support facilities for specific purposes.

These facilities are identified and located based on the requirements of the situation.

Incident size and complexity will influence the designation of facilities and locations.

Typical designated facilities include:

- Incident Command Post (ICP)
- Incident base
- Staging Areas
- Camps
- Mass casualty triage areas
- Points-of-distribution
- Emergency shelters

NIMS Management Characteristic: Comprehensive Resource Management

Maintaining accurate and up-to-date inventories of resources is an essential component of incident management.

Resources include personnel, equipment, teams, supplies, and facilities available or potentially available for assignment or allocation.

NIMS Management Characteristic: Integrated Communications

Integrated communications allow units from diverse agencies to connect, share information and achieve situational awareness.

Incident managers facilitate communications through the development and use of:

- A common communications plan
- Interoperable communications processes and systems
- Systems that include both voice and data links

Integrated Communications Planning occurs both before and during an incident to provide equipment, systems, and protocols needed to achieve integrated voice and data communications.

NIMS Management Characteristic: Establishment and Transfer of Command

When an incident is anticipated or occurs the organization with primary responsibility for the incident establishes command by designating the Incident Commander (IC) or Unified Command (UC). Command may need to be transferred to a different IC/UC one or more times over the course of a long duration or increasingly complex incident.

The current command determines the protocol for transferring command. This transfer process should always include a briefing for the incoming IC/UC on all essential information for continuing safe and effective operations. The transfer of command should also be communicated to all incident personnel.

NIMS Management Characteristic: Unified Command

In some incidents the Incident Command function is performed by a Unified Command (UC). UC is typically used for incidents involving:

- Multiple jurisdictions
- A single jurisdiction with multiagency involvement
- Multiple jurisdictions with multiagency involvement

UC allows agencies with different authorities and responsibilities to work together effectively without affecting individual agency authority, responsibility, or accountability.

NIMS Management Characteristic: Chain of Command and Unity of Command

Chain of command refers to the orderly command hierarchy within an incident management organization.

Unity of command means that each individual reports to only one designated supervisor.

These principles:

- Clarify reporting relationships
- Eliminate confusion caused by conflicting instructions
- Enable incident managers at all levels to direct the actions of all personnel under their supervision

NIMS Management Characteristic: Accountability

Accountability for all resources during an incident is essential.

Incident management personnel should adhere to principles of accountability, including:

- Check-in/checkout
- Incident action planning
- Unity of command
- Personal responsibility
- Span of control
- Resource tracking

NIMS Management Characteristic: Dispatch/Deployment

Resources should deploy only when requested and dispatched through established procedures by appropriate authorities.

Resources that authorities do not request should not deploy spontaneously - unrequested resources can overburden the IC/UC and increase accountability challenges.

NIMS Management Characteristic: Information and Intelligence Management

Incident-related information and intelligence is managed by the incident management organization through established processes for:

- Gathering
- Analyzing
- Assessing
- Sharing
- Managing

Information and intelligence management includes identifying essential elements of information (EEI). EEI ensures incident personnel gather the most accurate and appropriate data, translate it into useful information, and communicate it with appropriate personnel.

Visual 19:   Additional Resources

For more information, consult the following resources:

Visit this website to review the National Incident Management System (NIMS) - https://www.fema.gov/national-incident-management-system

- Visit this website to review HSPD-5 in its entirety - https://training.fema.gov/emiweb/is/icsresource/assets/hspd-5.pdf

Visit this website to review PPD-8 in its entirety - https://www.dhs.gov/presidential-policy-directive-8-national-preparedness

Visual 20:   Lesson Summary

You have completed the Course Overview lesson. The next lesson will describe how ICS is incorporated within the overall emergency management program.

Lesson 2: Incident Command and Unified Command

Visual 1:   Unit Objectives

At the end of this lesson, you should be able to:

- Describe chain of command and formal communication relationships.
- Identify common leadership responsibilities and values.
- Describe span of control and modular development.
- Describe the use of position titles.

Visual 2:   Chain of Command

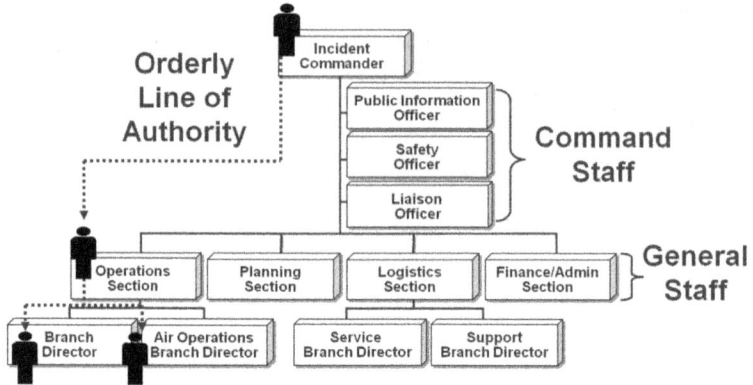

An orderly line of authority is used for the flow of task assignments and resource requests. This line of authority flows down through the organizational structure.

Visual 3:   Unity of Command

Unity of command means that each individual involved in incident operations will be assigned – and will report – to only one supervisor.

Chain of command and unity of command help to ensure that clear reporting relationships exist and eliminate the confusion caused by multiple, conflicting directives. Incident managers at all levels must be able to control the actions of all personnel under their supervision.

Unity of command clears up many of the potential communication problems encountered in managing incidents or events because each individual maintains a formal communication relationship only with his or her immediate supervisor.

Don't confuse unity of command with Unified Command!

Visual 4:   Unified Command (1 of 2)

When no one jurisdiction, agency, or organization has primary authority and/or the resources to manage an incident on its own, Unified Command may be established. There is no one "Commander." The Unified Command can allocate resources regardless of ownership or location.

This illustration shows three responsible agencies managing an incident together under a Unified Command.

Unified Command

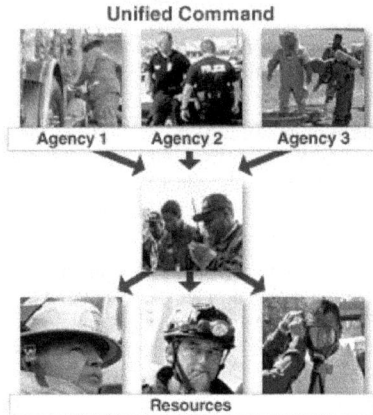

Agency 1   Agency 2   Agency 3

Resources

Visual 5:   Unified Command (2 of 2)

Unified Command:

- Enables all responsible agencies to manage an incident together by establishing a common set of incident objectives and strategies
- Allows Incident Commanders to make joint decisions by establishing a single command structure at one Incident Command Post (ICP)
- Maintains Unity of Command. Each employee reports to only one supervisor

Single ICP

Visual 6:   Advantages of Unified Command

Advantages of using Unified Command include:

- A single set of objectives guides incident response.
- A collective approach is used to develop strategies to achieve incident objectives.
- Information flow and coordination are improved between all involved in the incident.
- All agencies have an understanding of joint priorities and restrictions.
- No agency's legal authorities will be compromised or neglected.
- Agencies' efforts are optimized as they perform their respective assignments under a single Incident Action Plan.

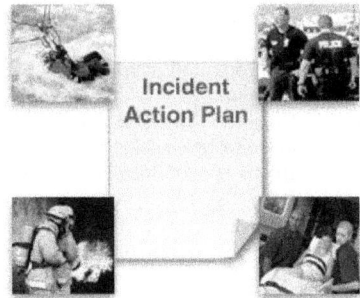

Incident Action Plan

Visual 7:   Activity 2.1: Unified Command

Activity Purpose: To practice recognizing potential incident management issues.

Time: 15 minutes

Instructions: Working with your team

1. Read the scenario in your Student Manual.
2. Identify the potential incident management issues.
3. List the incident management issues on chart paper.
4. Choose a spokesperson. Be prepared to present your findings to the class in 10 minutes.

Scenario:

A tornado collapsed a building, trapping 15 people in its basement. Fire department officers immediately designated a fire station located directly across from the incident site as the Incident Command Post (ICP). However, the fire station's confined location and immediate proximity to the incident made it ill-suited for directing the large-scale response effort. As police officers arrived on the scene, they decided to establish their Command Center at a school, several blocks away from the immediate response activities.

As response operations progressed and a mobile command vehicle became available, the Incident Command Post (ICP) was established in that vehicle just north of the hospital. Other agencies involved, such as the fire department and emergency medical services, began operating near the new ICP location and Incident Commander. The police department continued to operate from the school.

Activity 2.1: Unified Command

Activity 2.1: Unified Command

Activity Purpose: To practice recognizing potential incident management issues.

Time: 15 minutes

Instructions: Working with your team

1. Read the scenario in your Student Manual.
2. Identify the potential incident management issues.
3. List the incident management issues on chart paper.
4. Choose a spokesperson. Be prepared to present your findings to the class in 10 minutes.

Activity

Scenario:

A tornado collapsed a building, trapping 15 people in its basement. Fire department officers immediately designated a fire station located directly across from the incident site as the Incident Command Post (ICP). However, the fire station's confined location and immediate proximity to the incident made it ill-suited for directing the large-scale response effort. As police officers arrived on the scene, they decided to establish their Command Center at a school, several blocks away from the immediate response activities.

As response operations progressed and a mobile command vehicle became available, the Incident Command Post (ICP) was established in that vehicle just north of the hospital. Other agencies involved, such as the fire department and emergency medical services, began operating near the new ICP location and Incident Commander. The police department continued to operate from the school.

Visual 8:   Integrated Communications Overview

Formal communications follow the lines of authority. However, information concerning incident or event can be passed horizontally or vertically within the organization without restriction.

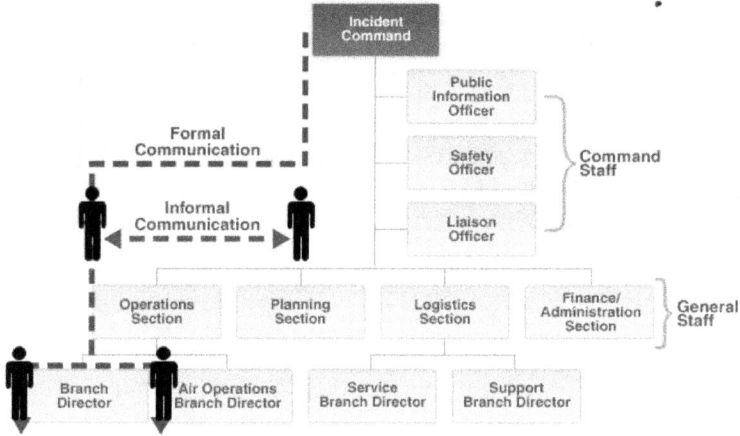

Full Organizational Chart description-Incident Command: Command Staff consists of the Public Information Officer, Safety Officer, and Liaison Officer; General Staff consists of Operations Section (Branch Director & Air Operations Branch Director), Planning Section, Logistics Section (Service Branch Director & Support Branch Director), Finance Section.

Visual 9:   Formal Communication

As illustrated on the previous screen, formal communication must be used when:

- Receiving and giving work assignments
- Requesting support or additional resources
- Reporting progress of assigned tasks

Other information concerning the incident or event can be passed horizontally or vertically within the organization without restriction. This is known as informal communication.

Visual 10:   Informal Communication

Informal communication:

- Is used to exchange incident or event information only
- Is NOT used for:
    - Formal requests for additional resources
    - Tasking work assignments

Within the ICS organization, critical information must flow freely!

Visual 11:   Informal Communication (Continued)

Examples of informal communication are as follows:

- The Communications Unit Leader may directly contact the Resources Unit Leader to determine the number of persons requiring communications devices.
- The Cost Unit Leader may directly discuss and share information on alternative strategies with the Planning Section Chief.

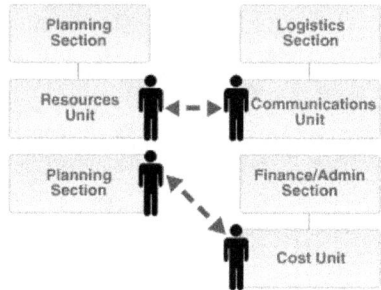

Visual 12:   Activity 2.2: Incident Communications

Activity Purpose: To practice identifying communication strategies to avoid problems during incident operations.

Time: 15 minutes

Instructions: Working with your team

1. Read the scenario in your Student Manual.
2. Identify strategies to address the communications problem.
3. List the strategies on chart paper.
4. Choose a spokesperson. Be prepared to present your findings to the class in 10 minutes.

Case Scenario:

Emergency communications at the Pentagon site proved challenging on September 11, 2001. Radio communications among emergency responders quickly became overloaded. These communication problems persisted throughout rescue operations. There was a need to record the identification number and location of each piece of equipment on the Pentagon grounds. Radio communications could not be employed to perform this task.

Activity 2.2 Incident Communications

Activity 2.2: Incident Communications

Activity Purpose: To practice identifying communication strategies to avoid problems during incident operations.

Time: 15 minutes

Instructions: Working with your team

1. Read the scenario in your Student Manual.
2. Identify strategies to address the communications problem.
3. List the strategies on chart paper.
4. Choose a spokesperson. Be prepared to present your findings to the class in 10 minutes.

Activity   **Case Scenario:**

Emergency communications at the Pentagon site proved challenging on September 11, 2001. Radio communications among emergency responders quickly became overloaded. These communication problems persisted throughout rescue operations. There was a need to record the identification number and location of each piece of equipment on the Pentagon grounds. Radio communications could not be employed to perform this task.

Visual 13:   Discussion Question

?

Why is leadership an essential element of successful incident/event management?

Visual 14:   Common Leadership Responsibilities

A good leader:

- **Communicates** by giving specific instructions and asking for feedback.
- **Supervises** the scene of action.
- **Evaluates** the effectiveness of the plan.
- **Understands and accepts** the need to modify plans or instructions.
- **Ensures** safe work practices.
- **Takes command** of assigned resources.
- **Motivates** with a "can do safely" attitude.
- **Demonstrates** initiative by taking action.

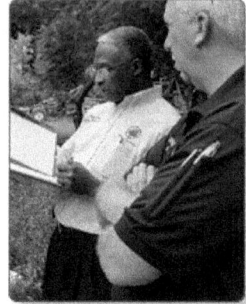

Note	The safety of all personnel involved in an incident or a planned event is the **first duty of ICS leadership.** This is the overall responsibility of Team Leaders, Group or Division Supervisors, Branch Directors, Sections Chiefs, and all members of the Command or Unified Command staff. Ensuring safe work practices is the top priority within the ICS common leadership responsibilities.

Visual 15:   Leadership & Values

A leader commits to excellence in all aspects of his or her professional responsibility. Leaders should know, understand, and practice the leadership responsibilities and recognize the relationship between these responsibilities and the leadership values. Commitment to duty, respect, and integrity are essential values that must be demonstrated in order for a leader to be effective.

Visual 16: Commitment to Duty

Duty begins with everything required by law and policy, but it is much more than simply fulfilling requirements.

How does an effective leader demonstrate commitment to duty to those he or she leads?

An effective leader should try to:

- Take charge within his or her scope of authority.
- Be prepared to step out of a tactical role to assume a leadership role.
- Be proficient in his or her job.
- Make sound and timely decisions.
- Ensure tasks are understood.
- Develop subordinates for future events.

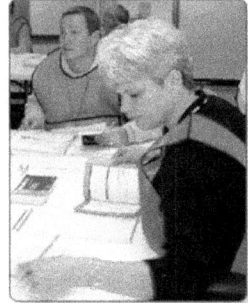

Visual 17:   Discussion Question

?

What can you do to demonstrate your commitment to duty to those you lead?

Visual 18:   Leadership & Respect

In order to maintain leadership and respect, a leader should:

- Know his or her subordinates and look out for their well-being. A leader's workforce is his or her greatest resource. Not all workers will succeed equally, but they all deserve respect.
- Keep his or her subordinates and supervisor informed by providing accurate and timely briefings and giving the intent behind assignments and tasks.
- Build the team. Conducting frequent briefings and debriefings with the team enables a leader to monitor progress and identify lessons learned. Considerations made during these meetings should include team experience, fatigue, and physical limitations when accepting assignments.

Visual 19:   Activity 2.3: Incident Leadership

Activity Purpose: To stimulate thought and discussion about desirable leadership qualities.

Time: 20 minutes

Instructions: Working with your team

1. Identify a highly effective incident leader you have known or know about.
2. List the main leadership qualities that such an individual must possess.
3. State how these qualities relate to leadership in incident response.
4. Choose a spokesperson. Be prepared to present your findings to the class in 5 minutes.

Activity 2.3 Incident Leadership

Activity 2.3: Incident Leadership

Activity Purpose: To stimulate thought and discussion about desirable leadership qualities.

Time: 20 minutes

Instructions: Working with your team

Activity

1. Identify a highly effective incident leader you have known or know about.
2. List the main leadership qualities that such an individual must possess.
3. State how these qualities relate to leadership in incident response.
4. Choose a spokesperson. Be prepared to present your findings to the class in 5 minutes.

Visual 20:   Communication Responsibilities

To ensure sharing of critical information, all responders must:

- Brief others as needed
- Debrief their actions
- Communicate hazards to others
- Acknowledge messages
- Ask if they do not know

While not always possible, the most effective form of communication is face-to-face.

Visual 21:　　Briefing Elements

Provide complete briefings that include clearly stated objectives and the following elements:

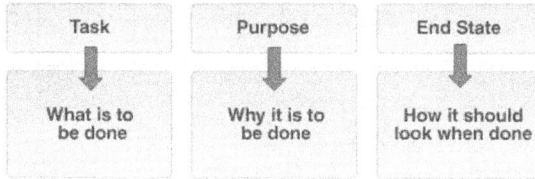

Task	Purpose	End State
↓	↓	↓
What is to be done	Why it is to be done	How it should look when done

Visual 22:   Incident Management Assessment

Assessment is an important leadership responsibility and is conducted after a major activity in order to allow employees and leaders to discover what happened and why. Assessment methods include:

- Corrective action report/After-Action Review (AAR)
- Debriefing
- Post-incident critique
- Mitigation plans

Visual 23:   Discussion Question

?

What questions would you use to assess the effectiveness of incident management?

Visual 24:   Using Common Terminology

ICS establishes common terminology that allows diverse incident management and support entities to work together.

Major functions and functional units with incident management responsibilities are named and defined. Terminology for the organizational elements involved is standard and consistent.

Visual 25:   ICS Organization: Review

The ICS organization:

- Is typically structured to facilitate activities in five major functional areas: Command, Operations, Planning, Logistics, and Finance/Administration
- Is adaptable to any emergency or incident to which domestic incident management agencies would be expected to respond
- Has a scalable organizational structure that is based on the size and complexity of the incident

However, this flexibility does NOT allow for the modification of the standard, common language used to refer to organizational components or positions.

ICS Organization: Review

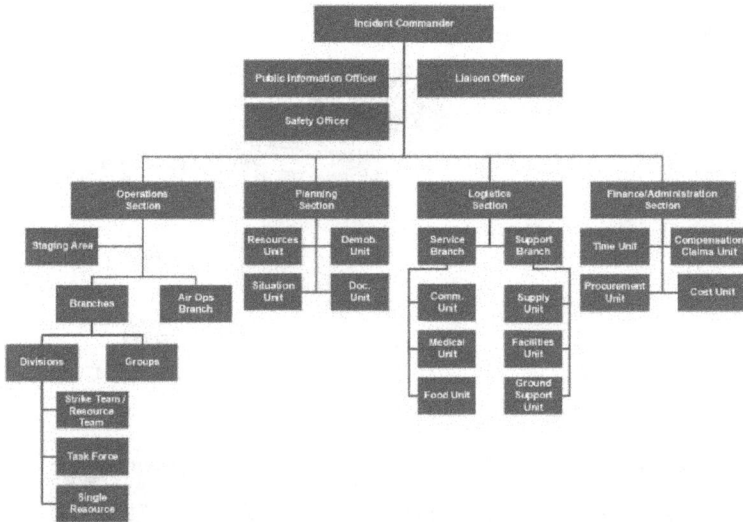

The ICS organizational chart shown above includes the following Command Staff: Incident Commander, Public Information Officer, Safety Officer, and Liaison Officer. General Staff includes the Operations, Planning, Logistics, and Finance/Admin. Sections.

Within the Operations Section there are two Branches. Subordinate to the Branches are Divisions and Groups. Under the Division there is a Strike Team, Task Force, and Single Resource.

Within the Planning Section the following Units are shown: Resources, Situation, Demobilization, and Documentation.

Within the Logistics Section two Branches are shown: the Service Branch with Communications, Medical, and Food Units, and the Support Branch with Supply, Facilities, and Ground Support Units.

Within the Finance/Admin. Section the following Units are shown: Time, Procurement, Compensation/Claims, and Cost.

Visual 26:   ICS Organization: Review (Continued)

Who's responsible for what?

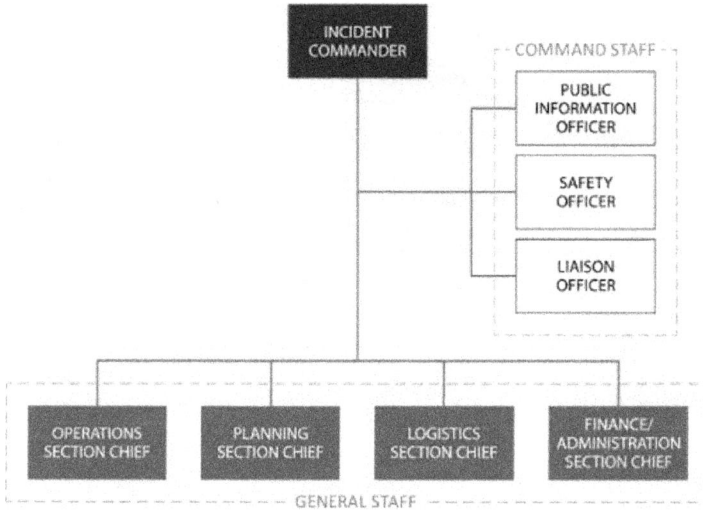

ICS Organization: Review (2 of 2) - ILT

Note

Standard Terminology Associated with Organizational Elements

- **Incident Commander (IC):** The individual responsible for all incident activities, including the development of strategies and tactics and the ordering and the release of resources. The IC has overall authority and responsibility for conducting incident operations and is responsible for the management of all incident operations at the incident site.
- **Command Staff:** The Command Staff consists of:
  - **Liaison Officer:** A member of the Command Staff responsible for coordinating with representatives from cooperating and assisting agencies. The Liaison Officer may have Assistants.
  - **Public Information Officer:** A member of the Command Staff responsible for interfacing with the public and media or with other agencies with incident-related information requirements.
  - **Safety Officer:** A member of the Command Staff responsible for monitoring and assessing safety hazards or unsafe situations, and for developing measures for ensuring personnel safety. The Safety Officer may have Assistants.
- **General Staff:** The organization level having functional responsibility for primary segments of incident management (Operations, Planning, Logistics, Finance/Administration). The Section level is organizationally between Branch and Incident Commander. Sections are as follows:
  - **Operations Section:** The Operations Section responsible for all tactical operations at the incident. The Operations Section includes:
    - **Branch:** That organizational level having functional, geographical, or jurisdictional responsibility for major parts of the incident operations. The Branch level is organizationally between Section and Division/Group in the Operations Section, and between Section and Units in the Logistics Section. Branches are identified by the use of Roman numerals, by function, or by jurisdictional name.
    - **Division:** That organization level having responsibility for operations within a defined geographic area. The Division level is organizationally between the Strike Team and the Branch.
    - **Group:** Groups are established to divide the incident into functional areas of operation. Groups are located between Branches (when activated) and Resources in

the Operations Section.

- **Unit:** That organization element having functional responsibility for a specific incident planning, logistics, or finance activity.
- **Task Force:** A group of resources with common communications and a leader that may be preestablished and sent to an incident or formed at an incident.
- **Strike Team/Resource Team:** Specified combinations of the same kind and type of resources, with common communications and a leader.
- **Single Resource:** An individual, a piece of equipment and its personnel complement, or an established crew or team of individuals with an identified work supervisor, that can be used on an incident.

- **Planning Section:** Responsible for the collection, evaluation, and dissemination of information related to the incident, and for the preparation and documentation of the Incident Action Plan. The Planning Section also maintains information on the current and forecasted situation, and on the status of resources assigned to the incident. This Section includes the Situation, Resources, Documentation, and Demobilization Units, as well as Technical Specialists.
- **Logistics Section:** The Section responsible for providing facilities, services, and materials for the incident. Includes the Service Branch (Communications Unit, Medical Unit, and Food Unit) and Support Branch (Supply Unit, Facilities Unit, and Ground Support Unit).
- **Finance/Administration Section:** The Section responsible for all incident costs and financial considerations. The Finance/Administration Section includes the Time Unit, Procurement Unit, Compensation/Claims Unit, and Cost Unit.
- **Intelligence/Investigations (I/I) Function:** Some incidents involve intensive intelligence gathering and investigative activity, and for such incidents, the Incident Commander or Unified Command may reconfigure intelligence and investigations responsibilities to meet the needs of the incident. The purpose of the Intelligence/Investigations function is to ensure that intelligence and investigative operations and activities are properly managed and coordinated.

Visual 27:   NIMS Management: Manageable Span of Control

The optimal span of control for incident management is one supervisor to five subordinates; however, effective incident management frequently necessitates ratios significantly different from this. The 1:5 ratio is a guideline, and incident personnel use their best judgment to determine the actual distribution of subordinates to supervisors for a given incident or EOC activation.

	Span of control is key to effective and efficient incident management. Maintaining an effective span of control is important because safety and accountability are a priority.
Note	

Visual 28:   Span of Control

?

What influences span of control?

Visual 29:   Modular Organization

The ICS organization adheres to a "form follows function" philosophy. The size of the current organization and that of the next operational period is determined through the incident planning process.

Because the ICS is a modular concept, managing span of control is accomplished by organizing resources into Teams, Divisions, Groups, Branches, or Sections. When the supervisor-to-subordinate ratio exceeds manageable span of control, additional Teams, Divisions, Groups, Branches, or Sections can be established. When a supervisor is managing too few subordinates, Sections, Branches, Divisions, Groups, or Teams can be reorganized or demobilized to reach a more effective span of control.

Visual 30:   Typical Organizational Structure

The initial response to most domestic incidents is
typically handled by local "911" dispatch centers,
emergency responders within a single jurisdiction, and
direct supporters of emergency responders. Most
responses need go no further.

Approximately 95% of all incidents are small
responses that include:

- Command: Incident Commander and other
  Command Staff
- Single Resource: An individual, a piece of
  equipment and its personnel complement, or
  an established crew or team of individuals with
  an identified work supervisor that can be used
  on an incident

Visual 31:   Expanding Incidents

Incidents that begin with single resources may rapidly expand requiring significant additional resources and operational support.

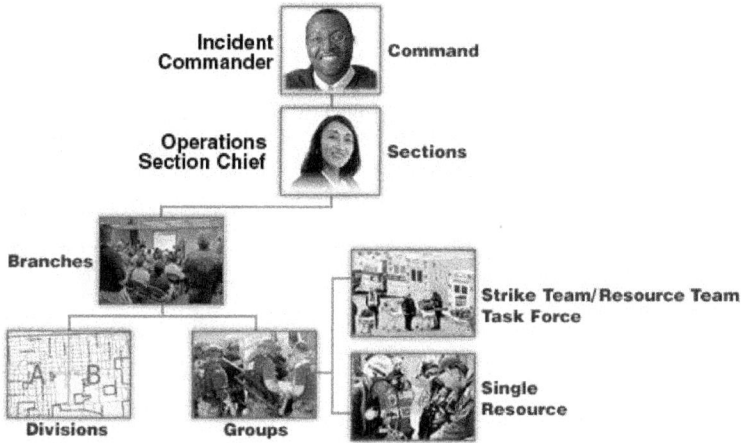

Visual 32:   Use of Position Titles

At each level within the ICS organization, individuals with primary responsibility positions have distinct titles. Using specific ICS position titles serves these important purposes:

- Provides a common standard
- Ensures qualified individuals fill positions
- Ensures that requested personnel are qualified
- Standardizes communication
- Describes the responsibilities of the position

Visual 33:   ICS Supervisory Position Titles

Titles for all ICS supervisory levels are shown in the table below:

Organizational Level	Title	Support Position
Incident Command	Incident Commander	Deputy
Command Staff	Officer	Assistant
General Staff (Section)	Chief	Deputy
Branch	Director	Deputy
Division/Group	Supervisor	N/A
Unit	Unit Leader	Manager
Strike Team/Task Force	Leader	Single Resource Boss

Visual 34:   Discussion Question

?

How you would adjust the organizational strategy to maintain span of control for the scenario below? Be sure to use proper principles, position titles, and features.

Scenario: The Command Staff consists of a Safety Officer and Public Information Officer. In the General Staff, the Operations Section has seven Strike Teams under the supervision of one Leader. Each Strike Team consists of a mix of different types of law enforcement and medical resources.

Visual 35:   Lesson Completion

You have completed the Incident Command and Unified Command lesson. You should now be able to:

- Describe chain of command and formal communication relationships.
- Identify common leadership responsibilities and values.
- Describe span of control and modular development.
- Describe the use of position titles.

The next lesson will discuss delegation of authority and management by objectives.

Lesson 3: Delegation of Authority & Management by Objectives

Visual 1:   Lesson 3 Overview

The Delegation of Authority & Management by Objectives lesson introduces you to the delegation of authority process, implementing authorities, management by objectives, and preparedness plans and agreements.

Lesson Objectives

At the end of this lesson, you should be able to:

- Describe the delegation of authority process.
- Describe scope of authority.
- Describe management by objectives.
- Describe the importance of preparedness plans and agreements.

Visual 2:   Delegation of Authority Process

Authority is a right or obligation to act on behalf of a
department, agency, or jurisdiction.

- In most jurisdictions, the responsibility for the protection
  of the citizens rests with the chief elected official.
  Elected officials have the authority to make decisions,
  commit resources, obligate funds, and command the
  resources necessary to protect the population, stop the
  spread of damage, and protect the environment.
- The Authority Having Jurisdiction (AHJ) is the entity
  that creates and administers processes to qualify, certify,
  and credential personnel for incident-related positions.
  AHJs include state, tribal, or Federal government
  departments and agencies, training commissions, NGOs,
  or companies, as well as local organizations such as
  police, fire, public health, or public works departments.
- In private industry, this same responsibility and authority
  rests with the chief executive officer.

Visual 3:   Discussion Question

?

Within your jurisdiction or agency, who has the authority for protecting citizens and responding to incidents?

Visual 4:   Scope of Authority

An Incident Commander's scope of authority is derived:

- From existing laws, agency policies, and procedures, and/or
- Through a delegation of authority from the agency administrator or elected official.

Visual 5:   Delegation of Authority

The process of granting authority to carry out specific functions is called the delegation of authority. Delegation of authority:

- Grants authority to carry out specific functions
- Is issued by the chief elected official, chief executive officer, or agency administrator in writing or verbally
- Allows the Incident Commander to assume command
- Does NOT relieve the granting authority of the ultimate responsibility for the incident

Ideally, this authority will be granted in writing. Whether it is granted in writing or verbally, the authorities granted remain with the Incident Commander until such time as the incident is terminated, or a relief shift Incident Commander is appointed, or the Incident Commander is relieved of his or her duties for just cause.

Agency Executive

Incident Commander

Visual 6:   Delegation of Authority: When Not Needed

A delegation of authority may not be required if the Incident Commander is acting within his or her existing authorities.

An emergency manager may already have the authority to deploy response resources to a small flash flood.

A fire chief probably has the authority (as part of the job description) to serve as an Incident Commander at a structure fire.

Visual 7:   Delegation of Authority: When Needed

A delegation of authority is needed:

- If the incident is outside the Incident Commander's jurisdiction
- When the incident scope is complex or beyond existing authorities
- If required by law or procedures

Visual 8:   Discussion Question

?

When would an Incident Commander in your jurisdiction or agency need a delegation of authority?

Visual 9:   Delegation of Authority: Elements

When issued, delegation of authority should include:

- Legal authorities and restrictions
- Financial authorities and restrictions
- Reporting requirements
- Demographic issues
- Political implications
- Agency or jurisdictional priorities
- Plan for public information management
- Process for communications
- Plan for ongoing incident evaluation

The delegation should also specify which incident conditions will be achieved prior to a transfer of command or release.

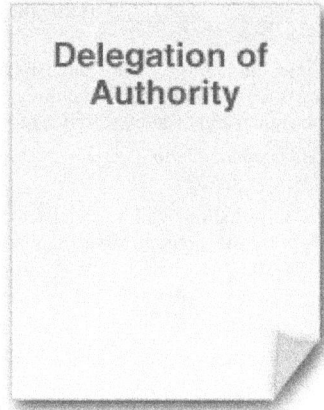

Delegation of Authority

Sample Delegation of Authority

_____ is assigned as Incident Commander on the _____ incident.

You have full authority and responsibility for managing the incident activities within the framework of agency policy and direction. Your primary responsibility is to organize and direct your assigned and ordered resources for efficient and effective control of the incident.

You are accountable to _____ or his/her designated representative listed below.

Financial limitations will be consistent with the best approach to the values at risk. Specific direction for this incident covering management and other concerns are:

1. Topic 1
2. Topic 2
3. Topic 3
4. etc.

_____ will represent me on any occasion that I am not immediately available. This authority is effective: _____.

_____
Agency Administrator

_____
Incident Commander

_____
Date and Time

Visual 10:   Discussion Question

?

How do you ensure that the delegating authority remains an active part of the incident response?

Visual 11:   Activity 3.1: Delegating Authority

Activity Purpose: To identify and reinforce ways that incident management personnel can keep their agency executives involved and informed during an incident.

Time: 15 minutes

Instructions: Working in your team:

1. Read the case study in your Student Manual.
2. Identify the steps you would take to keep the agency executives involved in this incident.
3. List the steps on chart paper.

Case Study:

The Beltway sniper case was one of the most infamous crimes in recent law enforcement, instilling fear in thousands of people. According to the after-action report, communication was clearly the most compelling concern in the sniper case. Investigations of this kind succeed or fail based on executives' ability to effectively manage and communicate information in a timely manner. Incident Commanders must balance the incident needs with the obligations of local executives to be responsive to their citizens. In the words of one police chief, "You cannot expect leaders to stop leading."

Activity 3.1: Delegating Authority

Activity 3.1: Delegating Authority

Activity Purpose: To identify and reinforce ways that incident management personnel can keep their agency executives involved and informed during an incident.

Time: 15 minutes

Instructions: Working in your team:

1. Read the case study in your Student Manual.
2. Identify the steps you would take to keep the agency executives involved in this incident.
3. List the steps on chart paper.

Activity   **Case Study:**

The Beltway sniper case was one of the most infamous crimes in recent law enforcement, instilling fear in thousands of people. According to the after-action report, communication was clearly the most compelling concern in the sniper case. Investigations of this kind succeed or fail based on executives' ability to effectively manage and communicate information in a timely manner. Incident Commanders must balance the incident needs with the obligations of local executives to be responsive to their citizens. In the words of one police chief, "You cannot expect leaders to stop leading."

Visual 12:   Implementing Authorities

Within their scope of authority, the Incident Commander establishes incident objectives, then determines strategies, resources, and ICS structure based on the incident objectives. The Incident Commander must also have the authority to establish an ICS structure adequate to protect the safety of responders and citizens, to control the spread of damage, and to protect the environment.

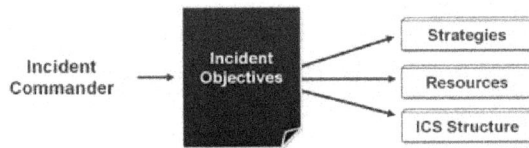

Visual 13:   Management by Objectives

ICS is managed by objectives. Objectives are communicated throughout the entire ICS organization through the Incident Action Planning Process.

Management by objectives includes:

- Establishing overarching objectives.
- Developing and issuing assignments, plans, procedures, and protocols.
- Establishing specific, measurable objectives for various incident management functional activities.
- Directing efforts to attain them, in support of defined strategic objectives.
- Documenting results to measure performance and facilitate corrective action.

Visual 14:   Establishing and Implementing Objectives

The steps for establishing and implementing incident objectives include:

- Step 1: Understand agency policy and direction.
- Step 2: Assess incident situation.
- Step 3: Establish incident objectives.
- Step 4: Select appropriate strategy or strategies to achieve objectives.
- Step 5: Perform tactical direction.
- Step 6: Provide necessary follow-up.

Incident Objectives

Visual 15:   Initial Response: Conduct a Size-Up

In an initial incident, a size-up is done to set the immediate incident objectives. The first responder to arrive must assume command and size-up the situation by determining:

- Nature and magnitude of the incident
- Hazards and safety concerns
    - Hazards facing response personnel and the public
    - Evacuation and warnings
    - Injuries and casualties
    - Need to secure and isolate the area
- Initial priorities and immediate resource requirements
- Location of Incident Command Post and Staging Area
- Entrance and exit routes for responders

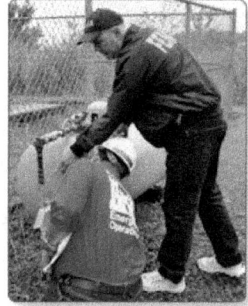

# Visual 16:	Overall Priorities

Throughout the incident, objectives are established based on the following priorities:

- First Priority: Life Safety
- Second Priority: Incident Stabilization
- Third Priority: Property Preservation

Overall priorities for an incident define what is most important. These are not a set of steps, you do not complete all life safety actions before you start any efforts to stabilize the incident. Often these priorities will be performed simultaneously.

Visual 17:   Effective Incident Objectives

For full effectiveness, incident objectives must be:

- Specific and state what's to be accomplished
- Measurable and include a standard and timeframe
- Attainable and reasonable
- In accordance with the Incident Commander's authorities
- Evaluated to determine effectiveness of strategies and tactics

EXAMPLE: *Establish a controlled perimeter around the incident within 45 minutes (by 6 p.m.)*

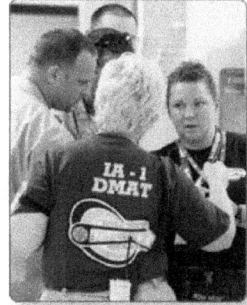

Visual 18:   Activity 3.2: Adding Incident Objectives

Activity Purpose: To give the students practice at developing incident objectives for a scenario.

Time: 20 minutes

Instructions: Working in your team:

1. Read the following scenario in your Student Manual.
2. Next, review the sample incident objectives
3. Determine what other incident objectives you would add for this incident.
4. List the objectives on chart paper and select a spokesperson.
5. Be prepared to present your additional objectives to the class in 5 minutes.

Scenario: At noon a sudden, severe windstorm strikes the city, uprooting trees, and trapping several commuters in their vehicles. Power is out to half of the city. Traffic is gridlocked. The storm has passed as quickly as it began.

Activity 3.2: Adding Incident Objectives

Activity 3.2: Adding Incident Objectives

Activity Purpose: To give the students practice at developing incident objectives for a scenario.

Time: 20 minutes

Instructions: Working in your team:

1. Read the following scenario in your Student Manual.
2. Next, review the sample incident objectives
3. Determine what other incident objectives you would add for this incident.
4. List the objectives on chart paper and select a spokesperson.
5. Be prepared to present your additional objectives to the class in 5 minutes.

Scenario: At noon a sudden, severe windstorm strikes the city, uprooting trees, and trapping several commuters in their vehicles. Power is out to half of the city. Traffic is gridlocked. The storm has passed as quickly as it began.

Activity

Visual 19:   Objectives, Strategies, and Tactics

Incident objectives, strategies, and tactics are three fundamental
pieces of a successful incident response.

- **Incident objectives** state what will be accomplished.
- **Strategies** establish the general plan or direction for
  accomplishing the incident objectives.
- **Tactics** specify how the strategies will be executed.

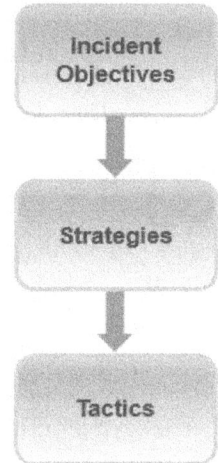

Visual 20:   Objectives, Strategies, and Tactics: Example

- **Objective:** Stop the spread of hazardous materials from a tractor-trailer accident into the river by 1800 today.
- **Strategy:** Employ barriers.
- **Tactic:** Use absorbent damming materials to construct a barrier between the downhill side of the accident scene and Murkey Creek.

The Incident Commander is responsible for establishing goals and selecting strategies. The Operations Section, if it is established, is responsible for determining appropriate tactics for an incident.

Visual 21:   Elements of an Incident Action Plan

An Incident Action Plan (IAP) covers an operational period and includes:

- What must be done
- Who is responsible
- How information will be communicated
- What should be done if someone is injured

The operational period is the period of time scheduled for execution of a given set of tactical actions as specified in the IAP.

Visual 22:   Operational Period Planning Cycle (Planning P)

The Incident Action Plan is completed each operational period utilizing the progression of meetings and briefings in the Operational Period Planning Cycle (Planning P). The Planning P is a graphical representation of the sequence and relationship of the meetings, work periods, and briefings that comprise the Operational Period Planning Cycle.

Visual 23:   Discussion Question

?

Given this objective and strategy, what tactic would you use if heavy rains are threatening to cause a dam break?

Objective: Decrease the probability of flooding by reducing the reservoir level to 35 feet by 0800 tomorrow.

Strategy: Pump water from reservoir.

Tactics: _____

Visual 24:   Preparedness Plans and Agreements

The Incident Commander, as well as the Command and General Staffs, should have a working knowledge of jurisdictional and agency preparedness plans and agreements.

Preparedness plans may take many forms. The most common preparedness plans are:

- Federal, State, or local Emergency Operations Plans (EOPs)
- Standard operating guidelines (SOGs) - a standard indication or outline of policy
- Standard operating procedures (SOPs) - a set of step-by-step instructions compiled by an organization to help workers carry out complex operations
- Jurisdictional or agency policies

Visual 25:   Emergency Operations Plan (EOP)

EOPs are developed at the Federal, State, and local levels to provide a uniform response to all hazards that a community may face.

EOPs should be consistent with the National Incident Management System (NIMS).

Visit this website to access the NIMS Resource Center: https://www.fema.gov/national-incident-management-system

Visit this website to access the Comprehensive Preparedness Guide (CPG) 101: A Guide for All-Hazard Emergency Operations Planning: https://www.fema.gov/pdf/about/divisions/npd/CPG_101_V2.pdf

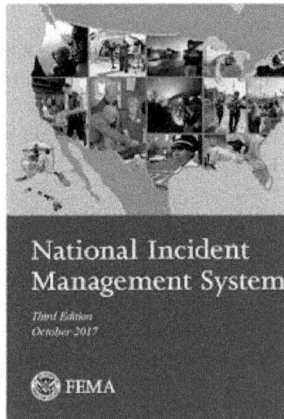

National Incident Management System

Third Edition
October 2017

FEMA

Visual 26:   Mutual Aid Agreements and Compacts

NIMS states that:

- Mutual aid agreements establish the legal basis for two or more entities to share resources. Mutual aid agreements may authorize mutual aid between two or more neighboring communities, among all jurisdictions within a state, between states, between Federal agencies, and/or internationally.
- Jurisdictions should be party to agreements with the appropriate jurisdictions and/or organizations from which they expect to receive, or to which they expect to provide, assistance.

Visit this website to review the Resource Management and Mutual Aid page within the NIMS Resource Center: https://www.fema.gov/resource-management-mutual-aid

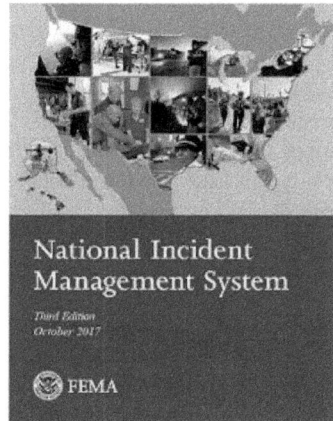

National Incident Management System

Third Edition
October 2017

FEMA

Visual 27:   Mutual Aid Agreements and Compacts (Continued)

Mutual aid is the voluntary provision of resources by agencies or organizations to assist each other when existing resources are inadequate.

NIMS resource management describes how mutual aid allows jurisdictions to share resources among mutual aid partners.

Note

Mutual Aid Agreement Topics

Mutual aid agreements might include some of the following topics:

- **Reimbursement:** Mutual aid services are either paid or unpaid (e.g., based on providing reciprocal services). Some mutual aid agreements specify reimbursement parameters.
- **Recognition of Licensure and Certification:** Guidelines to ensure recognition of licensures across geopolitical boundaries.
- **Procedures for Mobilization (Request, Dispatch, and Response):** Specific procedures for parties to request and dispatch resources through mutual aid.
- **Protocols for Voice and Data Interoperability:** Protocols that specify how different communications and IT systems share information.
- **Protocols for Resource Management:** Standard templates for packaging resources based on NIMS resource typing definitions and/or local inventory systems.

Visual 28:   Mutual Aid and Assistance: All Levels

Mutual aid agreements and assistance agreements are used at all
levels of government:

- Local jurisdictions participate in mutual aid through
  agreements with neighboring jurisdictions.
- States can participate in mutual aid through the
  Emergency Management Assistance Compact (EMAC).
- Federal agencies offer mutual aid to each other and to
  States, tribes, and territories under the National
  Response Framework (NRF).

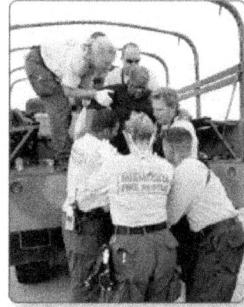

	Emergency Management Assistance Compact (EMAC)
Note	EMAC is a congressionally ratified mutual aid compact that defines a non-Federal, state-to-state system for sharing resources across state lines during an emergency or disaster. Signatories include all 50 states, the District of Columbia, Puerto Rico, Guam, and the U.S. Virgin Islands. EMAC's unique relationships with states, regions, territories, and Federal organizations, such as FEMA and the National Guard Bureau, enable it to move a wide variety of resources to meet the jurisdictions' needs.

Visual 29:   Information Derived from Plans

Plans may include information about:

- Hazards and risks in the area
- Resources in the area
- Other formal agreements and plans
- Contact information for agency administrators and response personnel
- Other pertinent information

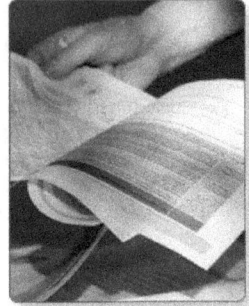

Visual 30:   Discussion Question

?

What preparedness plans, agreements, and standard operating procedures must you follow in responding to incidents?

Visual 31:   Lesson Completion

You have completed the Delegation of Authority & Management by Objectives lesson. You should now be able to describe:

- The delegation of authority process.
- Scope of authority.
- Management by objectives.
- The importance of preparedness plans and agreements.

The next lesson will discuss functional areas and positions.

Lesson 4: Functional Areas and Positions

Visual 1:   Lesson 4 Overview

The Functional Areas and Positions lesson introduces you to ICS organizational components, the Command Staff, the General Staff, and ICS tools.

Lesson Objectives

At the end of this lesson, you should be able to:

- Describe the functions of organizational positions within the Incident Command System (ICS).
- Identify the ICS tools needed to manage an incident.
- Demonstrate the use of an ICS Form 201.

This lesson provides more in-depth information on ICS organizational elements.

Visual 2:   Incident Commander

The Incident Commander:

- Has overall incident management responsibility delegated by the appropriate jurisdictional authority
- Develops the incident objectives to guide the Incident Action Planning Process
- Approves the Incident Action Plan and all requests pertaining to the ordering and releasing of incident resources

In some situations or agencies, a lower ranking but more qualified person may be designated as the Incident Commander. Whatever their day-to-day position, when a person is designated as the Incident Commander they are delegated the authority to command the incident response.

Visual 3:   Incident Commander (Continued)

The Incident Commander performs **all** major ICS functions unless he or she activates Command or General Staff positions to manage these functions. For example, the Incident Commander would personally perform the Operations function until an Operations Section was activated.

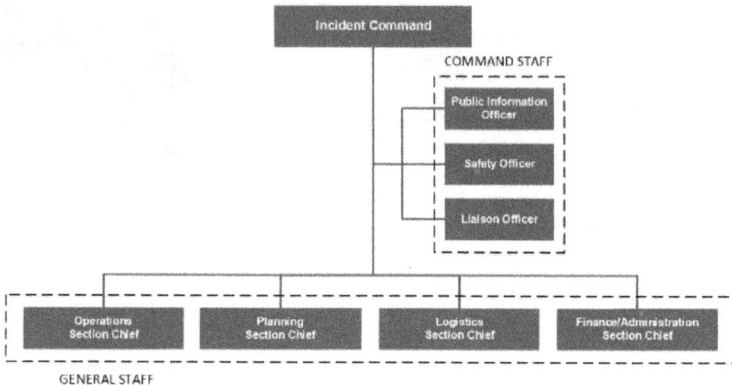

Visual 4:   Deputy Incident Commander

The Incident Commander may have one or more Deputies. Deputies may be assigned at the Incident Command, Section, or Branch levels. The only ICS requirement regarding the use of a Deputy is that the Deputy must be fully qualified and equally capable to assume the position.

The three primary reasons to designate a Deputy Incident Commander are to:

- Perform specific tasks as requested by the Incident Commander.
- Perform the incident command function in a relief capacity (e.g., to take over for the next operational period). In this case, the Deputy will assume the primary role.
- Represent an Assisting Agency that may share jurisdiction or have jurisdiction in the future.

Visual 5:   Command Staff

The Command Staff is only activated in response to the needs of the incident. If a Command Staff position is not needed it will not be activated. For example, an incident may not require a Liaison Officer if there are not outside agencies or organizations to coordinate with.

Command Staff includes the following positions:

- Public Information Officer
- Liaison Officer
- Safety Officer

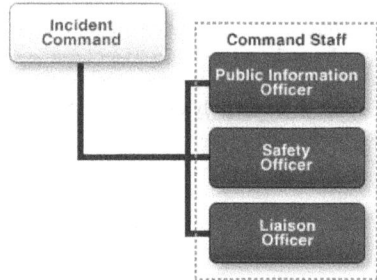

	Command Staff Functions
Note	The Incident Commander or Unified Command assigns Command Staff as needed to support the command function. The Command Staff typically includes a Public Information Officer (PIO), a Safety Officer, and a Liaison Officer who report directly to the Incident Commander or Unified Command and have assistants as necessary. The Incident Commander or Unified Command may appoint additional advisors as needed.

Visual 6:   Discussion Question

?

What are the major responsibilities of the Public Information Officer?

Visual 7:   Discussion Question

?

What are the major responsibilities of the Safety Officer?

Visual 8: Discussion Question

?

What are the major responsibilities of the Liaison Officer?

Command Staff Functions Table

Command Staff	Responsibilities
Public Information Officer (PIO)	The PIO interfaces with the public, media, and/or with other agencies with incident-related information needs. The PIO gathers, verifies, coordinates, and disseminates accessible,15 meaningful, and timely information on the incident for both internal and external audiences. The PIO also monitors the media and other sources of public information to collect relevant information and transmits this information to the appropriate components of the incident management organization. In incidents that involve PIOs from different agencies, the Incident Commander or Unified Command designates one as the lead PIO. All PIOs should work in a unified manner, speaking with one voice, and ensure that all messaging is consistent. The Incident Commander or Unified Command approves the release of incident-related information. In large-scale incidents, the PIO participates in or leads the Joint Information Center (JIC).
Safety Officer	The Safety Officer monitors incident operations and advises the Incident Commander or Unified Command on matters relating to the health and safety of incident personnel. Ultimate responsibility for the safe conduct of incident management rests with the Incident Commander or Unified Command and supervisors at all levels. The Safety Officer is responsible to the Incident Commander or Unified Command for establishing the systems and procedures necessary to assess, communicate, and mitigate hazardous environments. This includes developing and maintaining the incident Safety Plan, coordinating multiagency safety efforts, and implementing measures to promote the safety of incident personnel and incident sites. The

Command Staff	Responsibilities
	Safety Officer stops and/or prevents unsafe acts during the incident. Agencies, organizations, or jurisdictions that contribute to joint safety management efforts do not lose their individual responsibilities or authorities for their own programs, policies, and personnel. Rather, each contributes to the overall effort to protect all personnel involved in the incident.
Liaison Officer	The Liaison Officer is the incident command's point of contact for representatives of governmental agencies, jurisdictions, NGOs, and private sector organizations that are not included in the Unified Command. Through the Liaison Officer, these representatives provide input on their agency, organization, or jurisdiction's policies, resource availability, and other incident-related matters. Under either a single Incident Commander or a Unified Command structure, representatives from assisting or cooperating jurisdictions and organizations coordinate through the Liaison Officer. The Liaison Officer may have assistants.

Source: National Incident Management System (NIMS)

Visual 9:   Assistants

In a large or complex incident, Command Staff members may need one or more Assistants to help manage their workloads. Each Command Staff member is responsible for organizing his or her Assistants for maximum efficiency. Assistants are subordinates of principal Command Staff positions.

As the title indicates, Assistants should have a level of technical capability, qualifications, and responsibility subordinate to the primary positions.

Assistants may also be assigned to Unit Leaders (e.g., at camps to supervise unit activities).

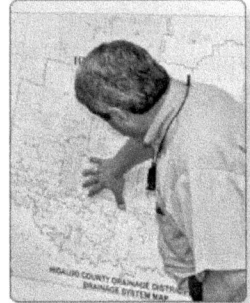

Visual 10:   Discussion Question

?

Scenario: On July 18, 2001, a train carrying hazardous chemicals derailed and caught fire in a downtown Baltimore tunnel, causing a near shutdown of the city and burning so hot that firefighters couldn't reach the flames for 8 hours.

At one point, all major highways into the city were blocked off, a Baltimore Orioles game at nearby Camden Yards was canceled, and the Inner Harbor was closed to boat traffic. A water-main break near the tunnel added to the chaos, causing the collapse of part of a major thoroughfare and power outages.

What is your recommended course of action?

Visual 11:   Assisting Agency

An agency or jurisdiction will often send resources to assist at an incident. In ICS these are called assisting agencies.

An assisting agency is defined as an agency or organization providing personnel, services, or other resources to the agency with **direct responsibility for incident management.**

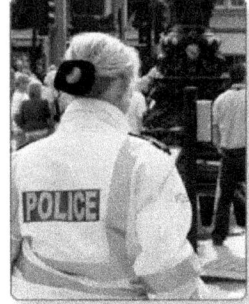

Visual 12:   Cooperating Agency

A cooperating agency is an agency **supplying assistance other than direct operational or support functions** or resources to the incident management effort.

Don't get confused between an assisting agency and a cooperating agency!

An assisting agency has direct responsibility for incident response, whereas a cooperating agency is simply offering assistance.

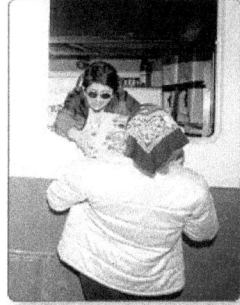

Visual 13:   Agency Representative

An Agency Representative is an individual assigned to an incident from an assisting or cooperating agency. The Agency Representative is delegated authority to make decisions on matters affecting that agency's participation at the incident.

Visual 14:   Expanding Incidents

An incident may start small and then expand. As the incident grows in scope and the number of resources needed increases, there may be a need to activate Teams, Units, Divisions, Groups, Branches, or Sections to maintain an appropriate span of control. The optimal span of control for incident management is one supervisor to five subordinates; however, effective incident management may require ratios different from this. The 1:5 ratio is just a guideline.

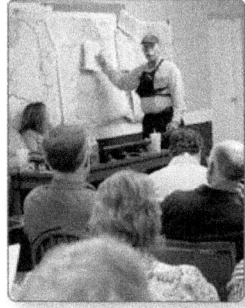

The ability to delegate the supervision of resources not only frees up the Incident Commander to perform critical decision-making and evaluation duties, but also clearly defines the lines of communication to everyone involved in the incident.

Next, we'll review the major organizational elements that may be activated during an expanding incident.

Visual 15:   Operations Section

The Operations Section:

- Directs and coordinates all incident tactical operations
- Is typically one of the first organizations to be assigned to the incident
- Expands from the bottom up
- Has the most incident resources
- May have Staging Areas and special organizations

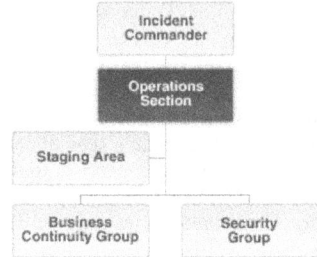

Visual 16:   Operations Section Chief

The Operations Section Chief:

- Is responsible to the Incident Commander for the direct management of all incident-related operational activities
- Establishes tactical objectives for each operational period
- Has direct involvement in the preparation of the Incident Action Plan

The Operations Section Chief may have one or more Deputies assigned. The assignment of Deputies from other agencies may be advantageous in the case of multijurisdictional incidents.

Operations
Section
Chief

Visual 17:   Operations Section: Staging Areas

Staging Areas are set up at the incident where resources can wait for a tactical assignment.

All resources in the Staging Area are assigned and ready for deployment. Out-of-service resources are NOT located at the Staging Area.

After a Staging Area has been designated and named, a Staging Area Manager will be assigned. The Staging Area Manager will report to the Operations Section Chief or to the Incident Commander if the Operations Section Chief has not been designated.

Visual 18:   Staging Areas: Chain of Command

The graphic below shows where the Staging Area Manager fits into the Operations Section.

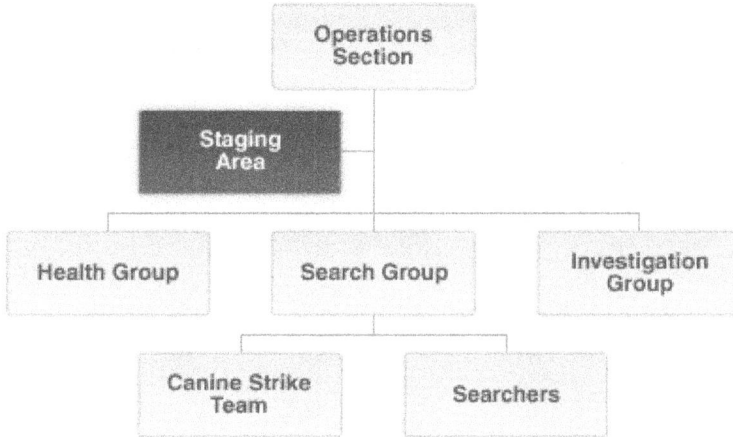

Visual 19:   Divisions and Groups

Divisions are established to divide an incident into physical or geographical areas of operation.

Groups are established to divide the incident into functional areas of operation.

For example, a Damage Assessment Task Force, reporting to the Infrastructure Group Supervisor, could work across divisions established to manage two distinct areas of the building that have been damaged — the west side of the building (West Division) and the north side (North Division).

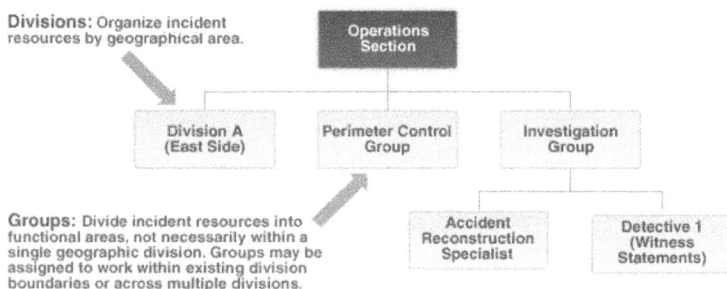

Divisions: Organize incident resources by geographical area.

Operations Section

Division A (East Side)

Perimeter Control Group

Investigation Group

Groups: Divide incident resources into functional areas, not necessarily within a single geographic division. Groups may be assigned to work within existing division boundaries or across multiple divisions.

Accident Reconstruction Specialist

Detective 1 (Witness Statements)

Visual 20:   Branches

Branches may be used to serve several purposes and may be functional or geographic in nature. Branches are established when the number of divisions or groups exceeds an effective span of control for the Operations Section Chief.

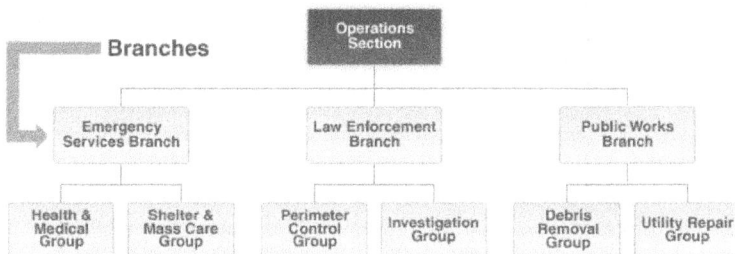

	Branches are identified by Roman numerals or functional name.
Note	Branches are managed by a Branch Director. Branch Directors may have deputy positions as required. In multiagency incidents, the use of Deputy Branch Directors from assisting agencies can be of great benefit to ensure and enhance interagency coordination.

Visual 21:   Activity 4.1: The Expanding Incident

Activity Purpose: To give students practice at maintaining span of control by adjusting the ICS organization structure as an expanding scenario incident unfolds.

Time: 30 minutes

Instructions: Working with your team . . .

1. Review the scenario.
2. Using an organization chart format, identify the supervisory structures (Divisions, Branches, Groups, Strike Teams, or Task Forces) that you would use to ensure a proper span of control for the resources currently on the scene.
3. For each organizational element, indicate the title of its supervisor.
4. Choose a spokesperson. Be prepared to present your organizational charts to the class in 15 minutes.

Scenario:

A swim meet is being held at the Main Street pool with 30 team members and 50 observers. During a race, a sudden electrical storm sends a lightning bolt into a flagpole near the pool and the charge arcs to the water. The pool is instantly electrified, sending guards and parents into the pool to rescue the children. The primary objectives are saving lives and ensuring safety.

On-Scene Resources: Local Police: 4 Marked Units; State Police: 2 Marked Units; Fire: 2 Engine Companies; Rescue: 1 Company; and EMS: 5 Basic Life Support and 2 Advanced Life Support

Activity 4.1: The Expanding Incident

Activity Purpose: To give students practice at maintaining span of control by adjusting the ICS organization structure as an expanding scenario incident unfolds.

Time: 30 minutes

Instructions: Working with your team . . .

1. Review the scenario.
2. Using an organization chart format, identify the supervisory structures (Divisions, Branches, Groups, Strike Teams, or Task Forces) that you would use to ensure a proper span of control for the resources currently on the scene.
3. For each organizational element, indicate the title of its supervisor.
4. Choose a spokesperson. Be prepared to present your organizational charts to the class in 15 minutes.

Activity

Scenario:

A swim meet is being held at the Main Street pool with 30 team members and 50 observers. During a race, a sudden electrical storm sends a lightning bolt into a flagpole near the pool and the charge arcs to the water. The pool is instantly electrified, sending guards and parents into the pool to rescue the children. The primary objectives are saving lives and ensuring safety.

On-Scene Resources: Local Police: 4 Marked Units; State Police: 2 Marked Units; Fire: 2 Engine Companies; Rescue: 1 Company; and EMS: 5 Basic Life Support and 2 Advanced Life Support

Visual 22:   Air Operations Branch

Some incidents may require the use of aviation resources to provide tactical or logistical support. On smaller incidents, aviation resources will be limited in number and will report directly to the Incident Commander or to the Operations Section Chief.

On larger incidents, it may be desirable to activate a separate Air Operations Branch to coordinate the use of aviation resources. The Air Operations Branch, will then report directly to the Operations Section Chief.

The Air Operations Branch Director can establish two functional groups. The Air Tactical Group coordinates all airborne activity. The Air Support Group provides all incident ground-based support to aviation resources.

Visual 23:   Planning Section

The Planning Section has responsibility for:

- Maintaining resource status
- Maintaining and displaying situation status
- Preparing the Incident Action Plan (IAP)
- Developing alternative strategies
- Providing documentation services
- Preparing the Demobilization Plan
- Providing a primary location for Technical Specialists assigned to an incident

One of the most important functions of the Planning Section is to look beyond the current and next operational period and anticipate potential problems or events.

Visual 24: Planning Section Key Personnel

The Planning Section will have a Planning Section Chief. The Planning Section Chief may have a Deputy.

Technical Specialists:

- Are advisors with special skills required at the incident
- Will initially report to the Planning Section, work within that Section, or be reassigned to another part of the organization
- Can be in any discipline required (e.g., epidemiology, infection control, chemical-biological-nuclear agents, etc.)

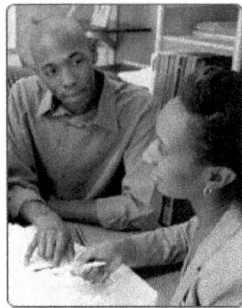

Visual 25:   Planning Section Units

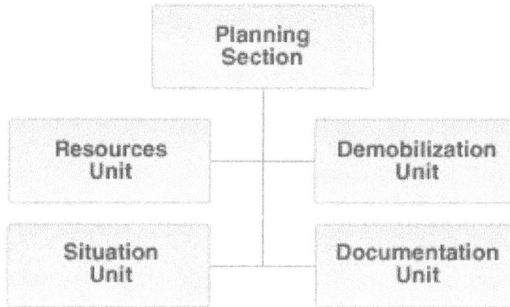

	Planning Section Units
Note	The major responsibilities of Planning Units are: • **Resources Unit:** Responsible for all check-in activity and for maintaining the status on all personnel and equipment resources assigned to the incident. • **Situation Unit:** Collects and processes information on the current situation, prepares situation displays and situation summaries, and develops maps and projections. • **Demobilization Unit:** On large, complex incidents, assists in ensuring that an orderly, safe, and cost-effective movement of personnel is made when they are no longer required at the incident. • **Documentation Unit:** Prepares the Incident Action Plan, maintains all incident-related documentation, and provides duplication services.

Visual 26:   Logistics Section

Early recognition of the need for a Logistics Section can reduce time and money spent on an incident. The Logistics Section is responsible for all support requirements, including:

- Communications
- Medical support to incident personnel
- Food for incident personnel
- Supplies, facilities, and ground support

Visual 27:   Logistics Section Units

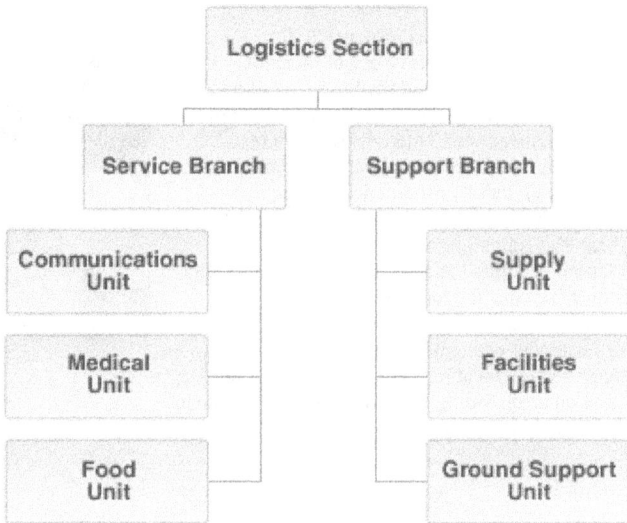

```
                          ┌─────────────────────┐
                          │  Logistics Section  │
                          └──────────┬──────────┘
                    ┌────────────────┴────────────────┐
          ┌──────────────────┐            ┌──────────────────┐
          │  Service Branch  │            │  Support Branch  │
          └──────────────────┘            └──────────────────┘
     ┌──────────────────┐                        ┌──────────────────┐
     │  Communications  │                        │     Supply       │
     │      Unit        │                        │      Unit        │
     └──────────────────┘                        └──────────────────┘
     ┌──────────────────┐                        ┌──────────────────┐
     │     Medical      │                        │    Facilities    │
     │      Unit        │                        │      Unit        │
     └──────────────────┘                        └──────────────────┘
     ┌──────────────────┐                        ┌──────────────────┐
     │      Food        │                        │  Ground Support  │
     │      Unit        │                        │      Unit        │
     └──────────────────┘                        └──────────────────┘
```

Note	**Logistics Section** It is important to remember that Logistics Section functions, except for the Supply Unit, are geared to supporting personnel and resources directly assigned to the incident. For example, the Medical Unit provides medical support to the incident response personnel. Medical resources that support the population affected by the incident would be managed under the Operations Section.

Visual 28:   Logistics Section: Service Branch

The Service Branch may be made up of the following units:

- The **Communications Unit** is responsible for developing plans for the effective use of incident communications equipment and facilities, installing and testing of communications equipment, supervision of the Incident Communications Center, distribution of communications equipment to incident personnel, and maintenance and repair of communications equipment.
- The **Medical Unit** is responsible for the development of the Medical Plan, obtaining medical aid and transportation for injured and ill incident personnel, and preparation of reports and records.
- The **Food Unit** is responsible for supplying the food needs for responder personnel for the entire incident, including all remote locations (e.g., Camps, Staging Areas), as well as providing food for personnel unable to leave tactical field assignments.

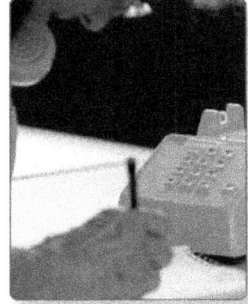

Visual 29:   Logistics Section: Support Branch

The Support Branch within the Logistics Section may include the following units:

- The **Supply Unit** is responsible for ordering personnel, equipment, and supplies; receiving and storing all supplies for the incident; maintaining an inventory of supplies; and servicing nonexpendable supplies and equipment.
- The **Facilities Unit** is responsible for setting up, maintaining, and demobilizing all facilities used in support of incident operations. Facilities Unit staff set up the Incident Command Post (ICP), Incident Base, and camps (including trailers or other forms of shelter in and around the incident area), ensure the maintenance of those facilities, and provide law enforcement/security services needed for incident support.
- The **Ground Support Unit** is responsible for supporting out-of-service resources; transporting personnel, supplies, food, and equipment; fueling, service, maintenance, and repair of vehicles and other ground support equipment; and implementing the Traffic Plan for the incident.

Visual 30:   Finance/Administration Section

The Finance/Administration Section:

- Is established when incident management activities require finance and other administrative support services.
- Handles claims related to property damage, injuries, or fatalities at the incident.

Remember that the ICS organizational structure is flexible and scalable to adapt to any situation. Not all incidents will require a separate Finance/Administration Section. If the full Finance/Administration Section is not needed, it would not be activated. When only one specific function is needed (e.g., cost analysis), a Technical Specialist assigned to the Planning Section could provide these services.

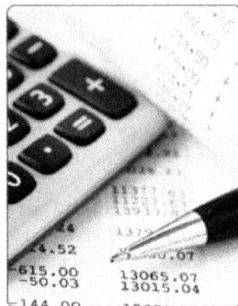

Visual 31:   Finance/Administration Units

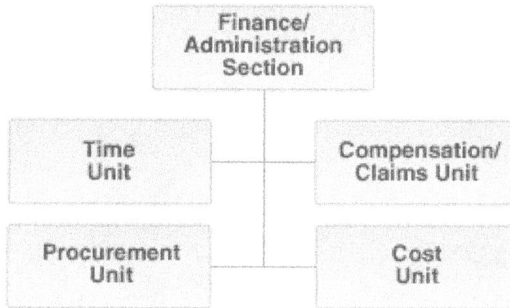

```
              ┌──────────────────┐
              │     Finance/     │
              │  Administration  │
              │     Section      │
              └────────┬─────────┘
        ┌──────────────┼──────────────┐
┌───────────────┐      │      ┌──────────────────┐
│     Time      │      │      │  Compensation/   │
│     Unit      │──────┼──────│   Claims Unit    │
└───────────────┘      │      └──────────────────┘
┌───────────────┐      │      ┌──────────────────┐
│  Procurement  │      │      │      Cost        │
│     Unit      │──────┴──────│      Unit        │
└───────────────┘             └──────────────────┘
```

Note	**Finance/Administration Units** Finance/Administration Units include the following: • The **Time Unit** is responsible for equipment and personnel time recording. • The **Procurement Unit** is responsible for administering all financial matters pertaining to vendor contracts, leases, and fiscal agreements. • The **Compensation/Claims** Unit is responsible for financial concerns resulting from property damage, injuries, or fatalities at the incident. • The **Cost Unit** is responsible for tracking costs, analyzing cost data, making cost estimates, and recommending cost-saving measures.

Visual 32:   Intelligence/Investigations Function in ICS

Intelligence/Investigations (I/I) is an ICS function identified in NIMS. When I/I is required for specialized types of responses, the IC/UC can place the I/I function in multiple locations within the incident command structure based on factors such as the nature of the incident, the level of I/I activity, and the relationship of I/I to other incident activities. The I/I can be placed in the Planning Section, in the Operations Section, within the Command Staff, as a separate General Staff section, or in some combination of these locations.

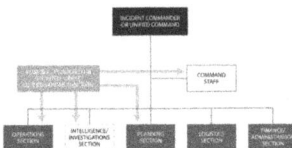

Visual 33:   Discussion Question

?

When might the I/I function be established as a branch under Operations? As a fifth General Staff Section within the ICS structure? As a part of the Command Staff?

Visual 34:   ICS Tools

Some important tools you should have available at the incident include:

- Emergency Operations Plan (EOP) from the affected jurisdiction(s)
- Agency policies and procedures manuals for responding agencies
- Maps of the affected area

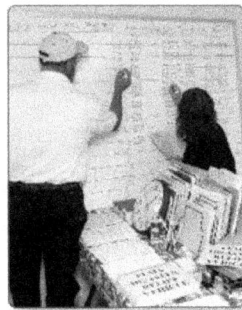

Visual 35:   ICS Forms

ICS Forms provide a method of recording and communicating key incident-specific information in a format that is simple, consistent, and supports interoperability. When using each ICS Form, you should ensure that you understand the following about each form:

- Purpose — What function does the form perform?
- Preparation — Who is responsible for preparing the form?
- Distribution — Who needs to receive this information?

Visual 36:   ICS Form 201, Incident Briefing

The Incident Briefing Form (ICS Form 201) is an eight-part form that provides an Incident Command/Unified Command with status information that can be used for briefing incoming resources, an incoming Incident Commander or team, or an immediate supervisor. The basic information includes:

- Incident situation (map, significant events)
- Incident objectives
- Summary of current actions
- Status of resources assigned or ordered for the incident or event

Incident Briefing Form

Visual 37: ICS Form 201, Incident Briefing (Continued)

Occasionally, the ICS Form 201 serves as the initial Incident Action Plan (IAP) until a Planning Section has been established and generates, at the direction of the Incident Commander, an IAP.

The ICS Form 201 is also suitable for briefing individuals newly assigned to the Command and General Staffs.

Incident Briefing Form

Visual 38:   Activity 4.2: Using ICS Form 201

Activity Purpose: To give students practice completing ICS Form 201 using information from a scenario incident.

Time: 60 minutes

Instructions: Working in your team:

1. Read the scenario on the following page of your Student Manual.
2. Complete the missing elements in the ICS Form 201, Incident Briefing, for the Emerald City Floods incident provided in your Student Manual, including:

   - Section 4 – Sketch: Identify and locate the incident facilities on the sketch provided.
   - Section 5 – Current Organization: Create an organizational chart for this incident.
   - Section 6 – Resource Summary:

     - Complete column 1 listing the resources ordered. (Base this list on the anticipated needs and incident objectives.)
     - In column 2, identify the resources by position, training level, or type.
     - In column 3, indicate if the resource is on scene or the time it should arrive.
     - In column 4, indicate the location where the resource is or will be assigned.

3. Choose a spokesperson to present your completed ICS Form 201. Be prepared to present your work in 30 minutes.

Activity 4.2: Using ICS Form 201

Activity Purpose: To give students practice completing ICS Form 201 using information from a scenario incident.

Time: 60 minutes

Instructions: Working in your team:

1. Read the scenario on the following page of your Student Manual.
2. Complete the missing elements in the ICS Form 201, Incident Briefing, for the Emerald City Floods incident provided in your Student Manual, including:

Activity

   - Section 4 – Sketch: Identify and locate the incident facilities on the sketch provided.
   - Section 5 – Current Organization: Create an organizational chart for this incident.
   - Section 6 – Resource Summary:

     - Complete column 1 listing the resources ordered. (Base this list on the anticipated needs and incident objectives.)
     - In column 2, identify the resources by position, training level, or type.

> - In column 3, indicate if the resource is on scene or the time it should arrive.
> - In column 4, indicate the location where the resource is or will be assigned.
>
> 3. Choose a spokesperson to present your completed ICS Form 201. Be prepared to present your work in 30 minutes.

Activity 4.2: Using ICS Form 201 Scenario

Status:

See map for projected inundation zone and impacted facilities. Floodwaters are projected to crest by 1800 3/15.

Initial Incident Objectives:

- Provide safety information and gear to personnel before they begin work assignments.
- Establish and publish schedule for press conferences by 1400.
- Evacuate vulnerable populations and areas of the city that may be cut off by floodwaters by 1800 today.
- Develop strategy to protect buildings and infrastructure from floodwaters by 1900 today.

Current Actions:

Activity

Command Post established in parking lot at Fire Station in Tactical Mobile Command Vehicle. Divisions A, B, C assigned to alert and warning in projected inundation zone; estimate completion by 1330. American Red Cross contacted to open shelter at Lafayette Middle School by 1400-briefed on evacuees from Lake Emerald Independent Living Center. Nursing Home and Lake Emerald Independent Living notified to implement evacuation plans not later than 1400. Lake Emerald confirms adequate transportation. City Water Authority notified to protect water treatment plant by 1600. Rapid River Nuclear Power Plant staff notified and implementing flood SOP by 1600. PIO has prepared public service announcement, awaiting approval by City Manager; press conference scheduled for 1330 at City Hall. Emerald City EOC in the process of being activated. County EOC in the process of being activated. Emerald City Hospital notified and prepared to receive Nursing Home evacuees by 1600. Resources ordered to support Water Treatment Plant Group and Nursing Home Evacuation Group. Edison Electric, Commonwealth Gas Co., and City Transit notified.

Weather:

Current weather pattern continues through midnight, then partial clearing. Highs in the mid 40s, lows in the high 30s. Chance of precipitation 60% through midnight, reducing to 40% after midnight. Expected precipitation next 24 hours 0.75 inches. Winds from the west 10-15 mph.

Safety Message:

Avoid skin contact with floodwaters. Drive with lights on. Watch for downed power lines in flood vicinity. Wear personal flotation devices when near/around water. Monitor City radio frequency F2 for safety updates.

Visual 39:   Other Commonly Used ICS Forms

Commonly used Incident Command System forms can be found on FEMA's Emergency Management Institute website for ICS Forms: FEMA's Emergency Management Institute website for ICS Forms

- ICS Form 202, Incident Objectives
- ICS Form 203, Organization Assignment List
- ICS Form 204, Assignment List
- ICS Form 205, Incident Radio Communications Plan
- ICS Form 206, Medical Plan •ICS Form 207, Organizational Chart
- ICS Form 208, Safety Message
- ICS Form 209, Incident Status Summary
- ICS Form 210, Status Change Card
- ICS Form 211, Check-In List
- ICS Form 213, General Message

- ICS Form 214, Unit Log
- ICS Form 215, Operational Planning Worksheet
- ICS Form 215a, Incident Action Plan Safety Analysis
- ICS Form 216, Radio Requirements Worksheet
- ICS Form 217, Radio Frequency Assignment Worksheet
- ICS Form 218, Support Vehicle Inventory
- ICS Form 220, Air Operations Summary
- ICS Form 221, Demobilization Plan
- ICS Form 308, Resource Order Form

Visual 40:   Lesson Completion

You have completed the Functional Areas and Positions lesson. You should now be able to:

- Describe the functions of organizational positions within the Incident Command System (ICS).
- Identify the ICS tools needed to manage an incident.
- Demonstrate the use of an ICS Form 201.

The next lesson will discuss briefings.

Lesson 5: Incident Briefings and Meetings

Visual 1:   Lesson 5 Overview

The Incident Briefings and Meetings lesson introduces you to different types of briefings and meetings.

Lesson Objectives

At the end of this lesson you should be able to:

- Describe components of field, staff, and section briefings/meetings.
- Prepare to give an Operational Period Briefing.

Visual 2: Incident Action Planning Process

The Incident Action Planning Process defines the progression of meetings and briefings utilized to develop the IAP that is used for the Operational Period Briefing. In addition to these IAP related meetings, there will also be other meetings and briefings within the ICS organization to include section-level meetings and briefings, situation update briefings, and transfer of command briefings.

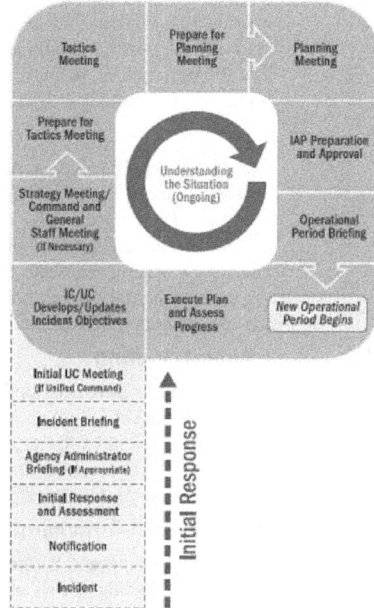

	Operational Period Planning Cycle
Note	**Initial Response and Assessment**

Initial Response and Assessment

The responder(s) who is first to arrive at the incident scene conducts the initial assessment and takes whatever immediate response actions are appropriate and possible. The initial or rapid assessment is essential to gaining and maintaining situational awareness. It enables the Incident Commander to request additional resources and/or support, develop, and implement initial tactics. Jurisdiction officials might decide to activate an EOC based on the initial assessment.

Agency Administrator Briefing

The Agency Administrator Briefing is a presentation to the personnel who will be managing or supporting the incident by the administrator or other senior official of the jurisdiction, agency, or organization affected by the incident. This briefing occurs when the Incident Commander or Unified Command are assuming duties outside their normal responsibilities or are from an entity or jurisdictional area that does not possess authority to the manage the incident they are being assigned. In such cases, the briefing provides supporting details to the delegation of authority or other document that the jurisdiction, agency, or organization typically provides to the Incident Commander or Unified Command.

During the briefing, the agency administrator or a designee provides information, guidance, and direction—including priorities and constraints— necessary for the successful management of the incident. The briefing is intended to ensure a common understanding between the jurisdiction, agency, or organization and the incident personnel regarding such things as the environmental, social, political, economic, and cultural issues relevant to the incident and its location.

Incident Briefing

The incident briefing marks the transition from reactive to proactive incident management. The initial responder(s) typically delivers the briefing to the incoming Incident Commander or Unified Command. This meeting enables the incoming Incident Commander or Unified Command to initiate planning for the next operational period.

Initial Unified Command Meeting

If a Unified Command is managing the incident, the Initial Unified Command Meeting allows members of the Unified Command to meet in private to discuss each jurisdiction or organization's priorities and objectives as well as any limitations, concerns, and restrictions. During the Initial Unified Command Meeting, members of the Unified Command generally accomplish the next step by developing the initial joint incident objectives.

Objectives Development/Update

The Incident Commander or Unified Command establishes the incident objectives for the initial operational period. After the initial operational period, the Incident Commander or Unified Command reviews the incident objectives and may validate them, modify them, or develop new objectives.

Incident objectives are based on incident priorities and other requirements. Clearly communicated priorities and objectives support unity of effort among incident personnel and enable the development of appropriate strategies and tactics. When the members of the team clearly understand the intent behind their instructions, they are better equipped to act decisively and make good decisions.

Strategy Meeting/Command and General Staff Meeting

After developing or revising the incident objectives, the Incident Commander or Unified Command typically meets with the Command and General Staff, and sometimes others, to discuss the incident objectives and provide direction. This meeting may be called the Strategy Meeting or the Command and General Staff Meeting and is held as needed to determine how best to meet the incident objectives.

The initial Strategy Meeting, which is held the first time through the planning cycle, is particularly important, because it allows team members to share information and jointly determine the initial approach to response operations. The initial Strategy Meeting may include the initial Incident Commander and a representative from the Agency Administrator.

Preparing for the Tactics Meeting

Once the approach to achieving or working toward achieving the incident objectives is determined, the Operations Section Chief and staff prepare for the Tactics Meeting by developing tactics and determining the resources that will be applied during the operational period.

Tactics Meeting

The Tactics Meeting is a forum for key players to review the proposed tactics developed by the Operations Section staff and to conduct planning for resource assignments. The Operations Section Chief leads the Tactics Meeting, and key participants include the Logistics Section Chief, Safety Officer, a representative from the Planning Section—typically, the Resources Unit Leader—and other technical specialists or team members invited by the Operations Section Chief, Logistics Section Chief, or Safety Officer. The team uses ICS Forms 215 and 215A, the Operational Planning Worksheet and the Incident Action Plan Safety Analysis, to facilitate and document decisions they make during the meeting.

Preparing for the Planning Meeting

Following the Tactics Meeting, preparations begin for the Planning Meeting. Team members collaborate between the Tactics Meeting and the Planning Meeting to identify support needs and assign specific operational resources to accomplish the operational plan.

Planning Meeting

The Planning Meeting serves as a final review and approval of operational plans and resource assignments developed during and after the Tactics Meeting. Ideally, the Planning Meeting involves no surprises and simply serves as a review of a plan that the Command and General Staff have collaboratively developed and agreed upon. At the end of the Planning Meeting, Command and General Staff, and any agency officials involved, confirm that they can support the plan.

Visual 3:   Effective Meetings and Briefings

Effective briefings and meetings are:

- An essential element to good supervision and incident management
- Intended to pass along vital information required in the completion of incident response actions

Typically, these briefings are concise and do not include long discussions or complex decision-making. Rather, they allow incident managers and supervisors to communicate specific information and expectations for the upcoming work period and to answer questions.

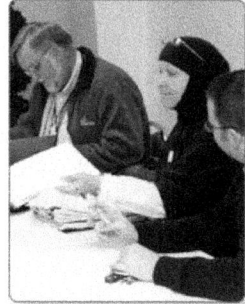

Visual 4:   Levels of Briefings

There are three types of briefings/meetings used in ICS: staff level, field level, and section level.

- **Staff-level briefings** are delivered to resources assigned to nonoperational and support tasks at the Incident Command Post or Base.
- **Field-level briefings** are delivered to individual resources or crews who are assigned to operational tasks and/or work at or near the incident site.
- **Section-level briefings** are delivered to an entire Section and include the **Operational Period Briefing.**

Note

Briefing Types

Staff-Level Briefings

This level typically involves resources assigned to nonoperational and support tasks that are commonly performed at the Incident Base or Command Post. These briefings will be delivered to individual staff members or full units within a section. These briefings occur at the beginning of the assignment to the incident and as necessary during the assignment. The supervisor attempts to clarify tasks and scope of the work as well as define reporting schedule, subordinate responsibilities and delegated authority, and the supervisor's expectations. The supervisor will also introduce coworkers and define actual workspace, sources of work supplies, and work schedule.

Field-Level Briefings

This level typically involves resources assigned to operational tasks and/or work at or near the incident site. These briefings will be delivered to individual subordinates, full crews, or multiple crews such as Strike Teams or Task Forces and will occur at the beginning of an operational shift. The location will usually be near the work site or just prior to mobilization to the field. The supervisor attempts to focus the subordinates on their specific tasks and helps define work area, reporting relationships, and expectations.

Section-Level Briefings

This level typically involves the briefing of an entire Section (Operations, Planning, Logistics, or Finance/Administration) and is done by the specific Section Chief. These briefings occur at the beginning of the assignment to the incident and after the arrival of Section supervisory staff. The Section

---

Chief may schedule periodic briefings at specific times (once per day) or when necessary. A unique briefing in this category is the **Operational Period Briefing** (also called a Shift Operations Briefing). Here, the Operations Section Chief presents the plan for all operational elements for the specific operational period. This specific briefing is done at the beginning of each operation shift and prior to the operational resources being deployed to the area of work. Often, a field-level briefing will take place subsequent to the completion of the Operational Period Briefing.

During any section-level briefing, the supervisor attempts to share incident-wide direction from the Incident Commander (IC), how the direction impacts the Section staff, and specific ways the Section will support the IC's direction. The supervisor will establish Section staffing requirements, Section work tasks, Section-wide scheduling rules, and overall timelines for meetings and completion of work products.

Visual 5:   Activity 5.1: Briefing Information

Activity Purpose: To give students practice at determining the appropriate details required when preparing for an incident briefing and identifying information pertinent to the audience to be covered in the briefing.

Time: 15 minutes

Instructions: Working in your group:

1. Review your assigned type of briefing (staff, field, section).
2. For the assigned type of briefing, list the specific types of information that you think should be in briefings. You may want to refer to the two previous visuals.
3. Choose a spokesperson to present your findings to the class. Be ready to present your list in 10 minutes.

Visual 6:   Briefing Topics Checklist

Below is a list of topics that you may want to include in a briefing.

- Current Situation and Objectives
- Safety Issues and Emergency Procedures
- Work Tasks
- Facilities and Work Areas
- Communications Protocols
- Supervisory/Performance Expectations
- Process for Acquiring Resources, Supplies, and Equipment
- Work Schedules
- Questions or Concerns

Activity 5.1: Briefing Information

Activity Purpose: To give students practice at determining the appropriate details required when preparing for an incident briefing and identifying information pertinent to the audience to be covered in the briefing.

Time: 15 minutes

Instructions: Working in your group:

Activity

1. Review your assigned type of briefing (staff, field, section).
2. For the assigned type of briefing, list the specific types of information that you think should be in briefings. You may want to refer to the two previous visuals.
3. Choose a spokesperson to present your findings to the class. Be ready to present your list in 10 minutes.

Visual 7:   Staff-Level Briefing Topics

Visual 8:   Field-Level Briefing

Visual 9:   Section-Level Briefing

Visual 10:   Operational Period Briefing

The Operational Period Briefing:

- Is conducted at the beginning of each operational period.
- Presents the Incident Action Plan for the upcoming period to supervisory personnel within the Operations Section.
- Should be concise.

In addition to the Operations Section Chief, the other members of the Command and General Staffs as well as specific support elements (i.e., Communications Unit, Medical Unit) can provide important information needed for safe and effective performance during the operational period.

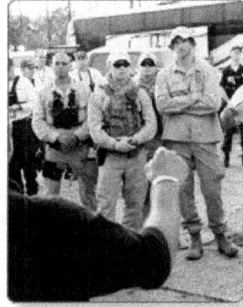

Visual 11:   Operational Period Briefing: Agenda

The Operational Period Briefing is facilitated by the Planning Section Chief and follows a set agenda. A typical briefing includes the following:

- The Planning Section Chief reviews the agenda and facilitates the briefing.
- The Incident Commander or Planning Section Chief presents incident objectives or confirms existing objectives.
- The Planning Section (Situation Unit Leader) provides information on the current situation.
- The current Operations Section Chief provides current assessment and accomplishments.
- The on-coming Operations Section Chief covers the work assignments and staffing of Divisions and Groups for the upcoming operational period.
- The Logistics Section Chief provides updates on transportation, communications, and supplies.
- The Finance/Administration Section Chief provides any fiscal updates.
- The Public Information Officer provides information on public information issues.
- The Liaison Officer briefs any interagency information.

Visual 12:   Operational Period Briefing: Agenda (Continued)

- Technical Specialists present updates on conditions affecting the response (weather, fire behavior, environmental factors).
- The Safety Officer reviews specific risks to operational resources and the identified safety/mitigation measures.
- Supervisors of specialized functions such as Intelligence/Investigations or Air Operations brief on their area (if activated).
- The Incident Commander reiterates his or her operational concerns and directs resources to deploy.
- The Planning Section Chief announces the next Planning Meeting and Operational Period Briefing, then adjourns the meeting.

Visual 13:   Activity 5.2: Operational Period Briefing

Activity Purpose: To give students practice at preparing and presenting briefings.

Time: 55 minutes

Instructions: Working in your team:

1. Prepare an operational period briefing using the information from the Emerald City Flood scenario begun in the previous units.
2. Include the following roles:

   - Incident Commander
   - Planning Section Chief
   - Operations Section Chief (assume no change of command)
   - Safety Officer
   - Weather Specialist

3. Be prepared to present your briefing in 20 minutes.

Activity 5.2: Operational Period Briefing

Activity Purpose: To give students practice at preparing and presenting briefings.

Time: 55 minutes

Instructions: Working in your team:

1. Prepare an operational period briefing using the information from the Emerald City Flood scenario begun in the previous units.
2. Include the following roles:

   - Incident Commander
   - Planning Section Chief
   - Operations Section Chief (assume no change of command)
   - Safety Officer
   - Weather Specialist

Activity   3. Be prepared to present your briefing in 20 minutes.

Debrief Instructions: Working in your team:

1. Monitor the time. After 20 minutes, Instructor will call time.
2. Teams will take turns presenting the briefings to each other:

- Round 1

  - Team 1 will present the operational period briefing.
  - Team 2 will participate as resources being briefed and ask questions as appropriate.

- Round 1 Feedback

  - Team 1 Self-Assessment: Team 1 will identify strengths of presentation and areas for improvement

- Team 2 Peer Feedback: Team 2 will provide constructive peer feedback.
- Instructor Feedback: Instructor will provide constructive feedback.
- Round 2
  - Reverse roles: Team 2 presents and Team 1 role plays the resources being briefed.

Visual 14: Lesson Completion

You have completed the Briefings lesson. You should now be able to:

- Describe components of field, staff, and section briefings/meetings.
- Prepare to give an Operational Period Briefing.

The next lesson will discuss organizational flexibility.

Lesson 6: Organizational Flexibility

Visual 1:   Lesson 6 Overview

The Organizational Flexibility lesson introduces you to flexibility within the standard ICS organizational structure.

Lesson Objectives

At the end of this lesson, you should be able to:

- Explain how the modular organization expands and contracts.
- Identify factors to consider when analyzing the complexity of an incident.
- Define the five types of incidents.

Visual 2:　　Flexibility and Standardization

A guiding principle of NIMS is **flexibility.** The ICS organization may be expanded easily from a very small size for routine operations to a larger organization capable of handling catastrophic events.

Standardization within ICS does NOT limit flexibility. ICS works for small, routine operations as well as catastrophic events.

Flexibility does NOT mean that the NIMS Management Characteristic Common Terminology is superseded. Flexibility is exercised only within the standard ICS organizational structure and position titles. Flexibility does not mean using non-standard organizational structures or position titles that would interfere with the NIMS Management Characteristics Common Terminology and Modular Organization.

Visual 3:   Modular Organization

Incident command organizational structure is based on:

- Size and complexity of the incident
- Specifics of the hazard environment created by the incident
- Incident planning process and incident objectives

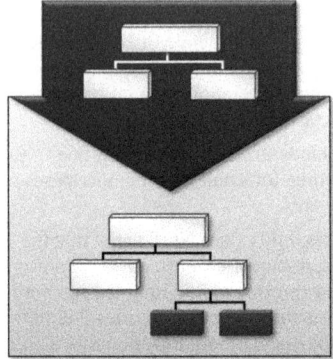

Visual 4:   Discussion Question

?

Should an incident's ICS organizational structure include all General and Command Staff functions and positions at all times?

Visual 5:   ICS Expansion and Contraction

Although there are no hard-and-fast rules, it is important to
remember that:

- Only functions and positions that are necessary to achieve
  incident objectives are filled.
- Each activated element must have a person in charge.
- An effective span of control must be maintained.

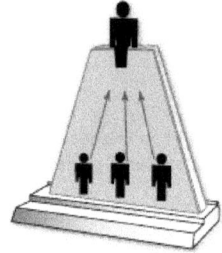

Visual 6:   Activation of Organizational Elements

Many incidents will never require the activation of the entire Command or General Staff or entire list of organizational elements within each Section. Other incidents will require some or all members of the Command Staff and all sub-elements of each General Staff section.

The decision to activate an element (Section, Branch, Division, Group or Unit) must be based on incident objectives and resource needs.

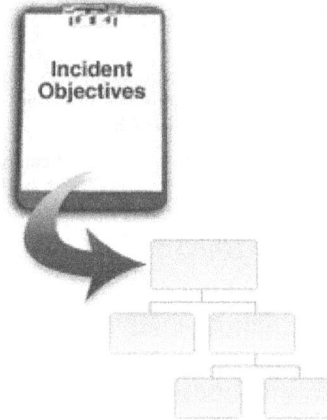

Visual 7:   Activation of Organizational Elements (Continued)

An important concept is that many organizational elements may be activated in various Sections **without** activating the Section Chief.

For example, the Situation Unit can be activated without a Planning Section Chief assigned. In this case, the supervision of the Situation Unit will rest with the Incident Commander.

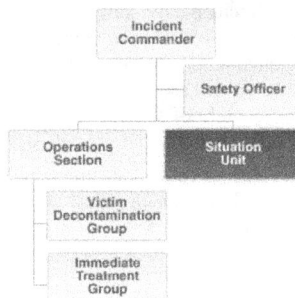

Incident Commander

Safety Officer

Operations Section

Situation Unit

Victim Decontamination Group

Immediate Treatment Group

Visual 8:   Discussion Question

?

Should you combine ICS positions and titles in order to save on staffing or achieve a higher level of efficiency?

Visual 9:   Avoid Combining Positions

It is tempting to combine ICS positions to gain staffing efficiency. Rather than combining positions, you may assign the same individual to supervise multiple units.

When assigning personnel to multiple positions, do not use nonstandard titles. Creating new titles may be unrecognizable to assisting or cooperating personnel and may cause confusion. Be aware of potential span-of-control issues that may arise from assigning one person to multiple positions.

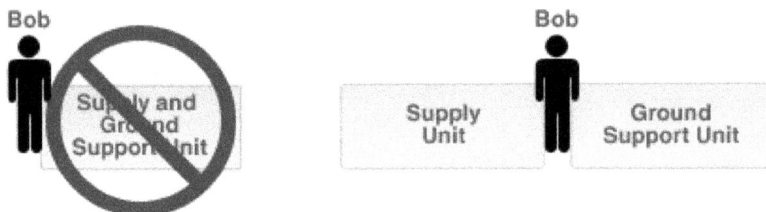

Visual 10:   Resource Management

Maintaining an accurate and up-to-date picture of resource utilization is a critical component of incident management. The incident resource management process consists of the following:

- Identifying Requirements
- Ordering and Acquiring
- Mobilizing
- Tracking and Reporting
- Demobilizing
- Reimbursing and Restocking

This section of the lesson reviews key resource management principles.

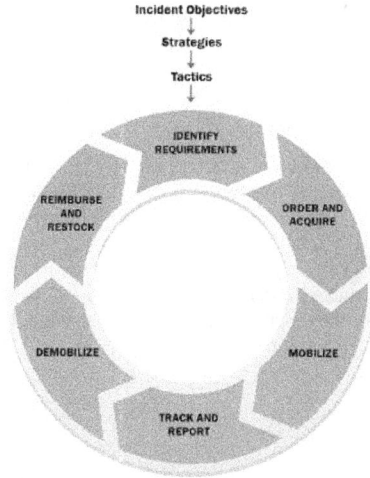

Visual 11:   Anticipating Incident Resource Needs

Experience and training will help you to predict workloads and corresponding staffing needs. As the graphic illustrates, an incident may build faster than resources can arrive.

Eventually, a sufficient number of resources arrive and begin to control the incident. As the incident declines, resources then exceed incident needs. Remember that when resources increase or decrease you will have to reassess your organizational structure and staffing to determine if it is right-sized for the resources that are being managed.

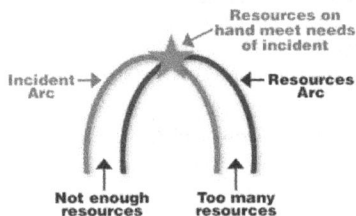

Visual 12:   Predicting Incident Workload

Incident workload patterns are often predictable throughout the incident life cycle. Several examples are provided below:

- **Operations Section:** The workload on Operations is immediate and often massive. On a rapidly escalating incident, the Operations Section Chief must determine appropriate tactics; organize, assign, and supervise resources; and at the same time participate in the planning process.
- **Planning Section:** The Resources and Situation Units will be very busy in the initial phases of the incident. In the later stages, the workload of the Documentation and Demobilization Units will increase.
- **Logistics Section:** The Supply and Communications Units will be very active in the initial and final stages of the incident.

Visual 13:   Analyzing Incident Complexity

It is important to strike the right balance when determining resource needs. Having too few resources can lead to loss of life and property, while having too many resources can result in unqualified personnel deployed without proper supervision.

A complexity analysis can help:

- Identify resource requirements
- Determine if the existing management structure is appropriate

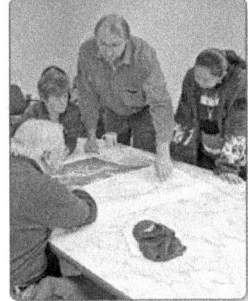

Visual 14:   Complexity Analysis Factors

- Community and responder safety
- Impacts to life, property, and the economy
- Potential hazardous materials
- Weather and other environmental influences
- Likelihood of cascading events
- Potential crime scene (including terrorism)
- Political sensitivity, external influences, and media relations
- Area involved, jurisdictional boundaries
- Availability of resources

Visual 15:   Activity 6.1: Complexity Analysis

Activity Purpose: To give the students practice at identifying the indicators that are considered when analyzing and determining the complexity of an incident.

Time: 20 minutes

Instructions: Working in your team:

1. Select an incident (e.g., flood, building collapse, water main break, bridge accident, hostage, hazardous materials, fire, disease outbreak, planned event, etc.). (Or you may want to assign an incident type to each team.)
2. Using the worksheet in the Student Manual (see the next page), identify a list of indicators that you might consider in order to determine the complexity of this incident. List the top three critical factors on chart paper.
3. Choose a spokesperson and be ready to present your complexity analysis to the class in 15 minutes.

Activity 6.1: Complexity Analysis

Activity Purpose: To give the students practice at identifying the indicators that are considered when analyzing and determining the complexity of an incident.

Time: 20 minutes

Instructions: Working in your team:

Activity

1. Select an incident (e.g., flood, building collapse, water main break, bridge accident, hostage, hazardous materials, fire, disease outbreak, planned event, etc.). (Or you may want to assign an incident type to each team.)
2. Using the worksheet in the Student Manual (see the next page), identify a list of indicators that you might consider in order to determine the complexity of this incident. List the top three critical factors on chart paper.
3. Choose a spokesperson and be ready to present your complexity analysis to the class in 15 minutes.

Activity 6.1: Complexity Analysis

Activity: Complexity Analysis Worksheet

Describe your selected incident (e.g., flood, building collapse, water main break, bridge accident).
List the specific indicators that you would use to analyze the complexity of this kind of incident.
Next, select your top three indicators.

Visual 16:   Incident Complexity and Resource Needs

As illustrated below, when incident complexity increases, your resource needs and ICS structure grow accordingly.

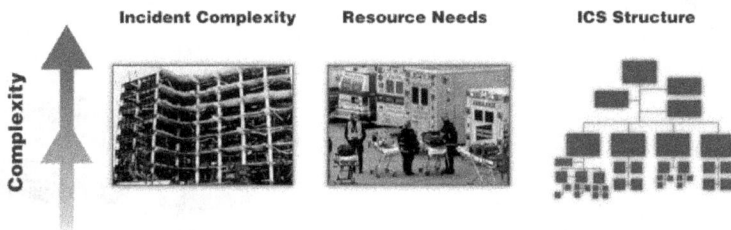

Visual 17:   Resource Typing

Resource Typing defines and categorizes incident resources by capability. Typing is done to ensure that responders get the right personnel and equipment.

ICS resources are categorized by Capability, Category, Kind, and Type.

- **Capability:** The Core Capability for which a resource is most useful.
- **Category:** The function for which a resource is most useful.
- **Kind:** A description of what a resource is (personnel, teams, facilities, equipment or supplies).
- **Type:** The resource's minimum capability to perform its function. The level of capability is based on size, power and capacity (for equipment), or experience and qualifications (for personnel or teams).

Kind = What's Needed?
Type = Qualifications? Capacities?

	Resource Typing Example
Note	Example: An Ambulance Ground Team is in the Emergency Medical Services **Category**. It's Resource **Kind** is a Team. The definition of a **Type 3 Ambulance Ground Team** includes a crew of 2 (an EMT 1 and an Ambulance Operator), with Basic Life Support (BLS) **Capability**, and the capacity to transport 2 non-ambulatory patients.

Visual 18:   Discussion Question

?

Which is a kind? Which is a type?
- Ordering a bus with seating for more than 40 adults is an example of ?
- Ordering a canine team is an example of ?

Visual 19: Importance of Resource Typing

Requesting a resource kind without specifying a resource type could result in an inadequate resource arriving on the scene.

The Order: "We need a HazMat team."

What You Needed   What Arrived

Visual 20: Resource Typing (Continued)

Resource types range from Type I (most capable) to Type IV (least capable), letting you reserve the appropriate level of resource for your incident by describing the size, capability, and staffing qualifications of a specific resource.

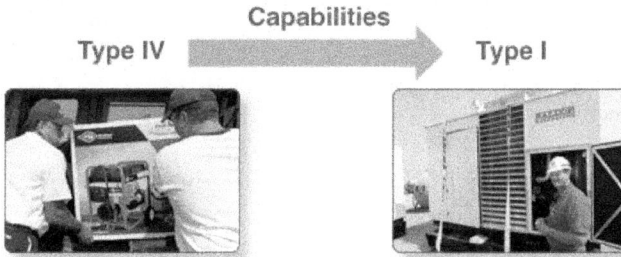

Visual 21:   Resource Typing and NIMS

Resource Management is a key component of NIMS. This effort helps all Federal, State, tribal, and local jurisdictions locate, request, and track resources to assist neighboring jurisdictions when local capability is overwhelmed.

The Resource Typing Library Tool (RTLT) is an online catalogue of national resource typing definitions, position qualifications and Position Task Books (PTBs) provided by the Federal Emergency Management Agency (FEMA).

For more information you can access the RTLT at https://rtlt.preptoolkit.fema.gov.

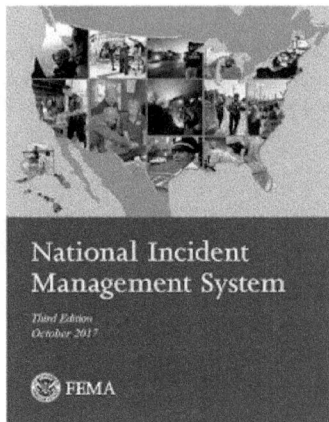

National Incident Management System

Third Edition
October 2017

FEMA

Visual 22:   Additional Resource Terminology

The following terms apply to resources:

- A **Task Force** is a combination of mixed resources with common communications operating under the direct supervision of a Task Force Leader.
- A **Strike Team / Resource Team** is a set number of resources of the same kind and type with common communications operating under the direct supervision of a Strike Team Leader. A Strike Team may also be referred to as a Resource Team by law enforcement.
- A **Single Resource** is an individual, a piece of equipment and its personnel complement, or a crew or team of individuals with an identified work supervisor that can be used on an incident.

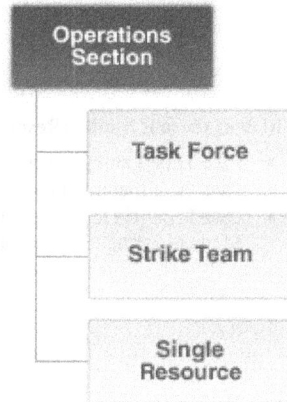

Visual 23:   Discussion Question

?

Which of these is Strike (Resource) Team? Task Force? Single Resource?

- Five Type I ambulances and crew complements with a leader.
- One Type I ambulance and crew complement.
- One Type III Helicopter, one Urban Search & Rescue Team, and one Emergency Medical Technician with a leader.

Visual 24: Incident Typing: Overview

Incidents, like resources, may be categorized into five types based on complexity. Type 5 incidents are the least complex and Type 1 the most complex. Incident typing may be used to:

- Make decisions about resource requirements.
- Order Incident Management Teams (IMTs). An IMT is made up of the Command and General Staff members in an ICS organization.

Type 1

Complexity

Type 5

Visual 25:   Incident Typing: Overview (Continued)

The incident type corresponds to both the number of resources required and the anticipated incident duration. The incident types move from Type 5 being the least complex to Type 1 being the most complex. As the number of resources required gets larger and the duration of the incident gets longer, the complexity increases. The vast majority of incidents are in the Type 3-5 range.

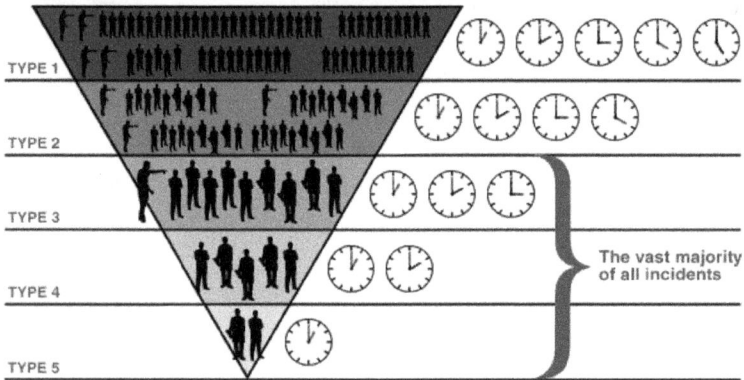

Clocks do not depict length of incident time.

Visual 26: Type 5 Incident

Characteristics of a Type 5 Incident are as follows:

- **Resources:** One or two single resources with up to six personnel. Command and General Staff positions (other than the Incident Commander) are not activated.
- **Time Span:** Incident is contained within the first operational period and often within a few hours after resources arrive on scene. No written Incident Action Plan is required.

Examples include a vehicle fire, an injured person, or a police traffic stop.

Visual 27:   Type 4 Incident

Characteristics of a Type 4 Incident are as follows:

- **Resources:** Command Staff and General Staff functions are activated (only if needed). Several single resources are required to mitigate the incident.
- **Time Span:** Limited to one operational period in the control phase. No written Incident Action Plan is required for non-HazMat incidents. A documented operational briefing is completed.

Visual 28:   Type 3 Incident

Characteristics of a Type 3 Incident are as follows:

- **Resources:** When capabilities exceed initial response, the appropriate ICS positions should be added to match the complexity of the incident. Some or all of the Command and General Staff positions may be activated, as well as Division or Group Supervisor and/or Unit Leader level positions. An Incident Management Team (IMT) or incident command organization manages initial action incidents with a significant number of resources, and an extended response incident until containment/control is achieved.
- **Time Span:** The incident may extend into multiple operational periods and a written Incident Action Plan may be required for each operational period.

Visual 29:   Type 2 Incident

Characteristics of a Type 2 Incident are as follows:

- **Resources:** Regional and/or national resources are required to safely and effectively manage the operations. Most or all Command and General Staff positions are filled. Operations personnel typically do not exceed 200 per operational period and the total does not exceed 500. The agency administrator/official is responsible for the incident complexity analysis, agency administrator briefings, and written delegation of authority.
- **Time Span:** The incident is expected to go into multiple operational periods. A written Incident Action Plan is required for each operational period.

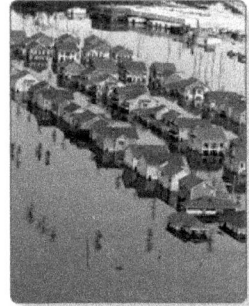

Visual 30:   Type 1 Incident

Characteristics of a Type 1 Incident are as follows:

- **Resources:** National resources are required to safely and effectively manage the operations. All Command and General Staff positions are activated, and Branches need to be established. Operations personnel often exceed 500 per operational period and total personnel will usually exceed 1,000. There is a high impact on the local jurisdiction, requiring additional staff for office administrative and support functions. The incident may result in a disaster declaration.
- **Time Span:** The incident is expected to go into multiple operational periods. A written Incident Action Plan is required for each operational period.

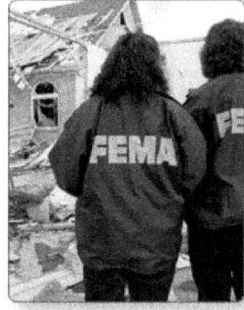

Visual 31:   Incident Management Teams (IMTs)

IMTs are rostered groups of ICS-qualified personnel consisting of an Incident Commander, other incident leadership, and personnel qualified for other key ICS positions. An IMT may be used to respond to an incident. IMTs include Command and General Staff members. IMT types correspond to incident type and include:

- Type 5: Local Village and Township Level
- Type 4: City, County, or Fire District Level
- Type 3: State, Territory, Tribal, or Metropolitan Area Level
- Type 2: National and State Level
- Type 1: National and State Level (Type 1 Incident)

Team members are certified as having the necessary training and experience to fulfill IMT positions.

Visual 32:   Activity 6.2: Incident Types

Activity Purpose: To give students practice at determining incident types for various scenarios.

Time: 15 minutes

Instructions: Working with your team:

1. Review the facts presented about the five incident scenarios in your Student Manual.
2. Determine the incident type.
3. Choose a spokesperson and be ready to list the incident types for each scenario in 10 minutes.

Note: A table summarizing characteristics of each type is provided after the scenarios.

IS-200.c Activity 6.2 Incident Types -

Activity 6.2: Incident Types

Activity Purpose: To give students practice at determining incident types for various scenarios.

Time: 15 minutes

Activity

Instructions: Working with your team:

1. Review the facts presented about the five incident scenarios in your Student Manual.
2. Determine the incident type.
3. Choose a spokesperson and be ready to list the incident types for each scenario in 10 minutes.

Note: A table summarizing characteristics of each type is provided after the scenarios.

Activity 6.2: Incident Types - Scenarios

Scenario 1:

- A multivehicle accident with critical injuries has occurred.
- Local resources are on the scene.
- The rescue and investigation should be complete in one operational period.
- The IAP is verbal.

Scenario 2:

- There is ongoing flooding in a tri-State area. o Local and regional resources are overwhelmed.
- There are numerous missing and injured persons.
- Additional rain and wind are forecasted.
- The President has declared all counties in the affected region as disaster areas under the Stafford Act.

Activity

Scenario 3:

- A cargo jet has crashed with injuries onboard and on the ground.
- Possible hazardous materials are aboard.
- State and local resources are managing the incident.
- All Command Staff positions are filled and the Operations and Planning Sections are being utilized.

Scenario 4:

- A small kitchen fire has occurred in a single family residence.
- The fire department, police and emergency medical services responded.

- The fire was out by the time the responders arrived on scene.
- The fire department confirmed the fire was out and helped the homeowner clear the smoke from the house.
- All units were back in service within one hour after the initial dispatch.

Scenario 5:

- A bank robber is holding staff and patrons hostage.
- An Operations Section has been activated with a Perimeter Control Group, Investigation Group, and SWAT Unit.
- The Command Staff includes the Incident Commander and a Public Information Officer.
- The incident may extend into multiple operational periods.

Activity 6.2: Incident Types

Incident Typing Review:

Incidents may be typed in order to make decisions about resource requirements. Incident types are based on the following five levels of complexity. (Source: U.S. Fire Administration)

Type 5	<ul><li>The incident can be handled with one or two single resources with up to six personnel.</li><li>Command and General Staff positions (other than the Incident Commander) are not activated.</li><li>No written Incident Action Plan (IAP) is required.</li><li>The incident is contained within the first operational period and often within an hour to a few hours after resources arrive on scene.</li><li>Examples include a vehicle fire, an injured person, or a police traffic stop.</li></ul>
Type 4	<ul><li>Command staff and general staff functions are activated only if needed.</li><li>Several resources are required to mitigate the incident, including a Task Force or Strike Team.</li><li>The incident is usually limited to one operational period in the control phase.</li><li>The agency administrator may have briefings, and ensure the complexity analysis and delegation of authority are updated.</li><li>No written Incident Action Plan (IAP) is required but a documented operational briefing will be completed for all incoming resources.</li><li>The role of the agency administrator includes operational plans including objectives and priorities.</li></ul>
Type 3	<ul><li>When capabilities exceed initial attack, the appropriate ICS positions should be added to match the complexity of the incident.</li></ul>

Type 5	• The incident can be handled with one or two single resources with up to six personnel. • Command and General Staff positions (other than the Incident Commander) are not activated. • No written Incident Action Plan (IAP) is required. • The incident is contained within the first operational period and often within an hour to a few hours after resources arrive on scene. • Examples include a vehicle fire, an injured person, or a police traffic stop.
	• Some or all of the Command and General Staff positions may be activated, as well as Division/Group Supervisor and/or Unit Leader level positions. • A Type 3 Incident Management Team (IMT) or incident command organization manages initial action incidents with a significant number of resources, an extended attack incident until containment/control is achieved, or an expanding incident until transition to a Type 1 or 2 IMT. • The incident may extend into multiple operational periods. • A written IAP may be required for each operational period.
Type 2	• This type of incident extends beyond the capabilities for local control and is expected to go into multiple operational periods. A Type 2 incident may require the response of resources out of area, including regional and/or national resources, to effectively manage the operations, command, and general staffing. • Most or all of the Command and General Staff positions are filled.

Type 5	• The incident can be handled with one or two single resources with up to six personnel. • Command and General Staff positions (other than the Incident Commander) are not activated. • No written Incident Action Plan (IAP) is required. • The incident is contained within the first operational period and often within an hour to a few hours after resources arrive on scene. • Examples include a vehicle fire, an injured person, or a police traffic stop.
	• A written IAP is required for each operational period. • Many of the functional units are needed and staffed. • Operations personnel normally do not exceed 200 per operational period and total incident personnel do not exceed 500 (guidelines only). • The agency administrator is responsible for the incident complexity analysis, agency administrator briefings, and the written delegation of authority.
Type 1	• This type of incident is the most complex, requiring national resources to safely and effectively manage and operate. • All Command and General Staff positions are filled. • Operations personnel often exceed 500 per operational period and total personnel will usually exceed 1,000. • Branches need to be established. • The agency administrator will have briefings, and ensure that the complexity analysis and delegation of authority are updated. • Use of resource advisors at the incident base is recommended.

Type 5	• The incident can be handled with one or two single resources with up to six personnel. • Command and General Staff positions (other than the Incident Commander) are not activated. • No written Incident Action Plan (IAP) is required. • The incident is contained within the first operational period and often within an hour to a few hours after resources arrive on scene. • Examples include a vehicle fire, an injured person, or a police traffic stop.
	• There is a high impact on the local jurisdiction, requiring additional staff for office administrative and support functions.

Visual 33:   Lesson Completion

You have completed the Organizational Flexibility lesson. You should now be able to:

- Explain how the modular organization expands and contracts.
- Identify factors to consider when analyzing the complexity of an incident.
- Define the five types of incidents.

The next lesson will cover transfer of command.

Lesson 7: Transfer of Command

Visual 1:   Lesson 7 Overview

The Transfer of Command lesson introduces you to transfer of command briefings and procedures.

Lesson Objectives

At the end of this lesson you should be able to:

- Describe the process of transfer of command.
- List the briefing elements involved in transfer of command.

Visual 2:   Transfer of Command

Transfer of command is the process of moving the responsibility for incident command from one Incident Commander to another.

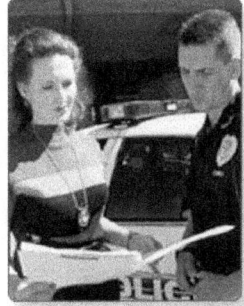

Visual 3:   When Command Is Transferred

Transfer of command may take place for many reasons, including when:

- A jurisdiction or agency is legally required to take command
- Change of command is necessary for effectiveness or efficiency
- Incident complexity changes
- There is a need to relieve personnel on incidents of extended duration
- Personal emergencies arise (e.g., Incident Commander has a family emergency)
- The Agency Administrator or Jurisdictional Executive directs a change in command

Visual 4:   Discussion Question

?

If a more qualified person arrives on the scene, does this mean a change in incident command must occur? Why or Why not?

Visual 5:   A More Qualified Person Arrives

The arrival of a more qualified person does NOT necessarily mean a change in incident command.

The more qualified individual may:

- Assume command according to agency guidelines
- Maintain command as it is and monitor command activity and effectiveness
- Request a more qualified Incident Commander from the agency with a higher level of jurisdictional responsibility

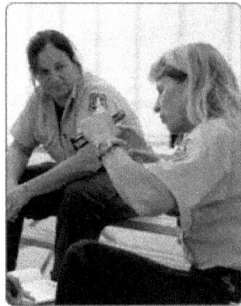

Visual 6:   Transfer of Command Procedures

One of the main features of ICS is a procedure to transfer command with minimal disruption to the incident. This procedure may be used any time personnel in supervisory positions change.

Whenever possible, transfer of command should:

- Take place face-to-face
- Include a complete briefing that captures essential information for continuing safe and effective operations

The effective time and date of the transfer of command should be communicated to all personnel involved in the incident.

Visual 7:   Discussion Question

?

What would you include in a transfer of command briefing?

Visual 8:   Transfer of Command Briefing Elements

A transfer of command briefing should always take place. The briefing should include:

- Situation status
- Incident objectives and priorities
- Current organization
- Resource assignments
- Resources ordered and en route

- Incident facilities
- Incident communications plan
- Incident prognosis, concerns, and other issues
- Introduction of Command and General Staff members

Visual 9:   Incident Briefing Form (ICS Form 201)

Agency policies and incident-specific issues may alter the transfer of command process. In all cases, the information shared must be documented and saved for easy retrieval during and after the incident.

The initial Incident Commander can use the ICS Form 201 to document actions and situational information.

For more complex transfer of command situations, every aspect of the incident must be documented and included in the transfer of command briefing.

Incident
Briefing Form

Visual 10:   Activity 7.1: Transfer of Command

Activity Purpose: To give students the opportunity to identify the elements that should be included in a transfer of command briefing.

Time: 10 minutes

Instructions: Working individually:

1. Review the Emerald City Flood update provided in your Student Manual.
2. Review the list of briefing elements and check the items that should be included in the transfer of command briefing.
3. Be prepared to share your answer in 5 minutes.

Incident Update: Let's return to the Emerald City Incident. It is now 1800 and the water level is still rising. You are relieving the current Incident Commander for the next operational period. Review the list below and check the items that should be included in the transfer of command briefing.

IS-200.c Activity 7.1 - Transfer of Command

Activity 7.1: Transfer of Command

Activity Purpose: To give students the opportunity to identify the elements that should be included in a transfer of command briefing.

Time: 10 minutes

Instructions: Working individually:

Activity

1. Review the Emerald City Flood update provided in your Student Manual.
2. Review the list of briefing elements and check the items that should be included in the transfer of command briefing.
3. Be prepared to share your answer in 5 minutes.

Incident Update: Let's return to the Emerald City Incident. It is now 1800 and the water level is still rising. You are relieving the current Incident Commander for the next operational period. Review the list below and check the items that should be included in the transfer of command briefing.

Activity 7.1: Transfer of Command

Transfer of Command Activity

Briefing Element	Yes	No
Situation Status		
Incident Objectives and Priorities		
Current Organization		
Current Expenditures and Anticipated Budget		
Resource Assignment		
Resources En Route or On Order		
Incident Facilities		

Briefing Element	Yes	No
Incident Communications Plan		
News Releases and Media Monitoring Reports		
Incident Prognosis		
Special Requests from Agency Representatives		
Introduction of Command and General Staff Members		

Visual 11:   Lesson Completion

You have completed the Transfer of Command lesson. You should now be able to:

- Describe the process of transfer of command.
- List the briefing elements involved in transfer of command.

The next lesson will be an activity that provides practice in applying the concepts discussed in this course.

Lesson 8: Application Activity

Visual 1:   Lesson 8: Application Activity

Lesson Objectives

At the end of this lesson, you should be able to apply key concepts in a scenario-based activity:

- NIMS Management Characteristics
- Incident Command and Unified Command
- Initial Size-up
- Developing Incident Objectives
- Determining Resource Requirements
- Determining Appropriate ICS Structure for an Incident
- Transfer of Command

Visual 2:   Scenario: Liberty County

Liberty County Map

The scenario for this activity takes place in Liberty County.

Liberty County is located in the fictional State of Columbia, on the Atlantic Coast between Canada and Mexico.

Liberty County is primarily rural with large tracts of forests, grazing lands and farmlands.

The population of the county is 302,412. Almost half of the population resides in Central City, and another quarter of the county's permanent residents live in four smaller cities: Fisherville, Harvest Junction, Kingston and Bayport.

Liberty County government includes a Sheriff's Department, Emergency Management Center, Public Health Department, Public Works Department and Board of Schools. The county infrastructure includes a dam and reservoir, a seaport and two airports.

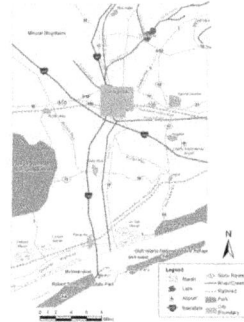

Scenario: Liberty County

Liberty County Map

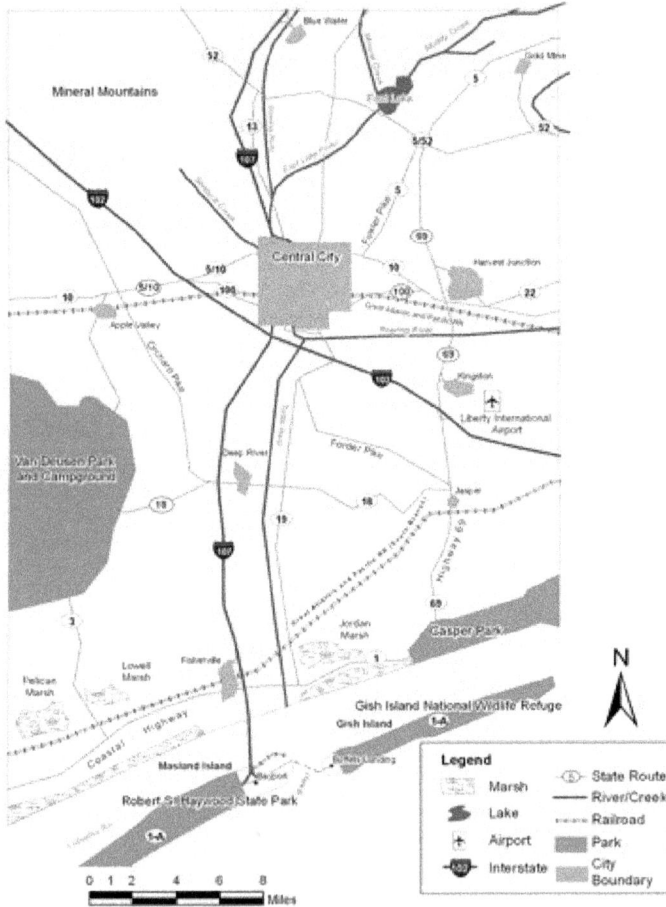

Visual 3:   Central City

Central City is the county seat for Liberty County and houses a population of 149,000. It is a diverse city with industrial areas, commercial areas, multi-family housing complexes and single family sub-divisions.

Central City government includes a Fire Department, Police Department, and Public Works Department. The city has a separate school district, four hospitals and two universities.

Central City

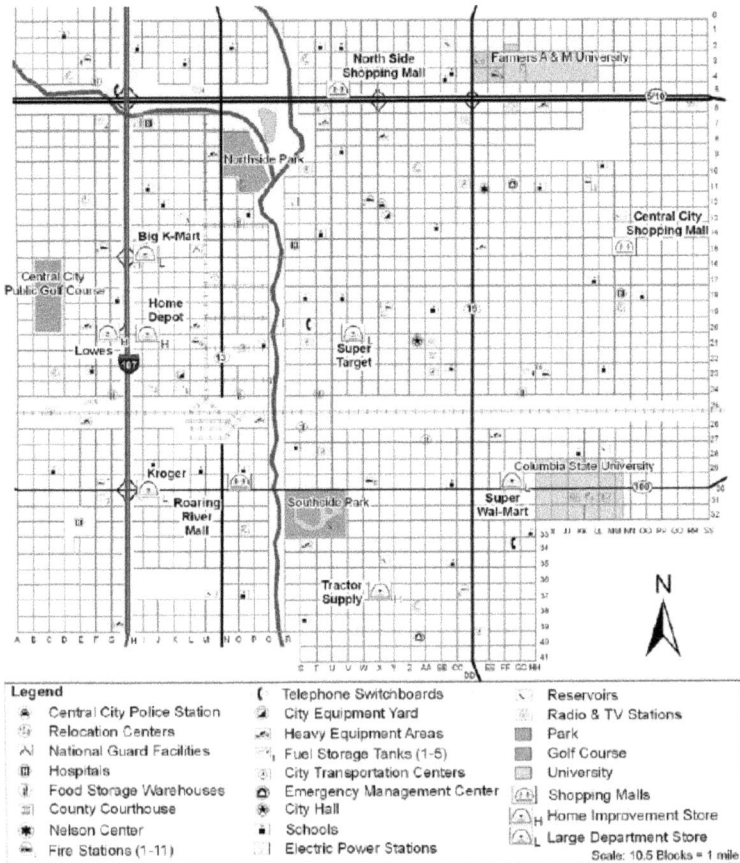

Legend

⚘ Central City Police Station	(Telephone Switchboards	⬩ Reservoirs
☺ Relocation Centers	☑ City Equipment Yard	Radio & TV Stations
N National Guard Facilities	Heavy Equipment Areas	Park
⊞ Hospitals	Fuel Storage Tanks (1-5)	Golf Course
Food Storage Warehouses	City Transportation Centers	University
County Courthouse	Emergency Management Center	Shopping Malls
✳ Nelson Center	☀ City Hall	Home Improvement Store
Fire Stations (1-11)	Schools	Large Department Store
	Electric Power Stations	Scale: 10.5 Blocks = 1 mile

Visual 4:   Your Role

You are a member of the emergency management
community within Liberty County and Central City.

You could be from any of the many disciplines that
could be involved in response to an incident, such as
Fire, Police, Emergency Medical Services, Public
Works, or Public Health. For the purposes of
this activity, it is not important.

You are the first supervisory level person arriving
on the scene of an incident. In this activity, you will
apply what you have learned in this course to choose
the appropriate initial response action that should
occur.

Visual 5: Liberty County Fairgrounds

The Liberty County Fairgrounds are located northwest of Central City. Fairgrounds Avenue, the southern boundary of the fairgrounds, is one street north of the city limits, within the jurisdiction of Liberty County.

The indoor and outdoor facilities at the Liberty County Fairgrounds are utilized throughout most of the year.

Visual 6:   Liberty County Fair and Rodeo

It is the week of the annual Liberty County Fair and
Rodeo. This event is hosted at the fairgrounds and
attracts several thousands of visitors daily.

Early in the evening large crowds fill the 127-acre
complex. People stream to and from the parking areas;
traffic is congested; and the Midway area, outdoor
stage, and Grandstand are filled to capacity.

Small elements of the County Sheriff's office, the
Central City Police Department, the Central City Fire
Department, and County Emergency Medical Services
(EMS) are located in and around the fairgrounds to
provide for public safety at the event. These
organizations are operating cooperatively, but no
centralized incident command structure has been
established.

Visual 7:   Tanker Truck Crash

At about 5 p.m. A large truck traveling fast heading west on Fairgrounds Avenue veers off the road, jumps the curb near the fairgrounds entrance, and passes through the crowd. The vehicle stops when it runs into an exhibit hall next to the outdoor stage. A few moments later, as the crowd begins to react, the large truck catches fire.

Several people were injured as the tanker truck passed through the crowd and there could be deaths. There is disorder as some attempt to flee and others try to help.

The large truck is an active fire that must be suppressed and could spread to nearby structures. There are other potential hazards including a damaged building and utilities (power, water, and gas) that could be damaged.

Public safety personnel on scene- law enforcement, fire, and EMS- respond immediately to the incident. Both the Central City and Liberty County Emergency Operations Centers are notified of these events and prepare to send any additional resources required for the incident.

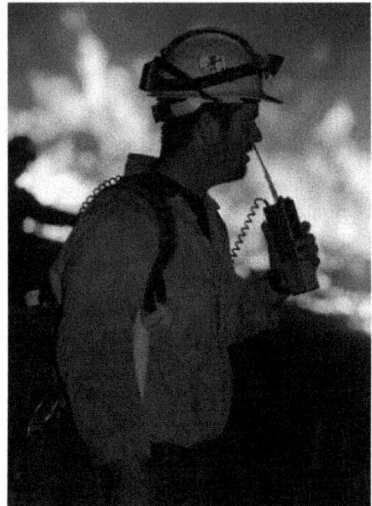

Visual 8:   Establish Command

It is now approximately 5:15 pm. You are the first supervisor on scene and there is a need to quickly to establish Incident Command.

Let's review a few of the NIMS Management Characteristics that apply to determining the best approach for the Incident Command function in an incident:

- **Establishment and Transfer of Command** - the first on scene need to explicitly establish incident or unified command and clearly state and record when command is transferred.
- **Chain of Command and Unity of Command** - all responders must be under a single command structure led by a designated Incident Commander (IC) or Unified Command (UC).
- **Unified Command** - if multiple organizations, disciplines, or jurisdictions are involved in the response, is a single IC sufficient, or is there a need for a unified command? UC is normally used for incidents involving multiple jurisdictions, a single jurisdiction with multiagency involvement, or multiple jurisdictions with multiagency involvement.

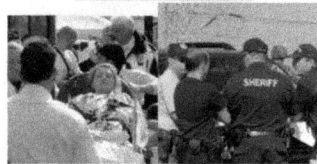

Visual 9:   Activity 8.1: Establish Command

Activity Purpose: To apply key concepts regarding establishing command.

Time: 10 minutes

Instructions: Working with your team . . .

1. Review the scenario on the previous screens.
2. Consider the following - You are the first supervisor on scene - what type of incident command do you think is needed?
3. Choose a spokesperson. Be prepared to present your answer to the class in 10 minutes.

Activity 8.1: Establish Command

Activity Purpose: To apply key concepts regarding establishing command.

Time: 10 minutes

Instructions: Working with your team . . .

Activity

1. Review the scenario on the previous screens.
2. Consider the following - You are the first supervisor on scene - what type of incident command do you think is needed?
3. Choose a spokesperson. Be prepared to present your answer to the class in 10 minutes.

Visual 10:   Establish Command (Continued)

You have established incident command under a single Incident Commander. This Incident Commander will be from the Central City Fire Department. Other jurisdictions and agencies involved in response to this incident will take their direction from this Incident Commander.

This conforms to the NIMS Management Characteristic of **Chain of Command and Unity of Command** – all responders are under a single command structure led by an Incident Commander.

Remember that the Incident Commander will manage the incident by establishing a common set of incident objectives for all jurisdictions and agencies involved in this response.

Incident Commander

Visual 11:   So, what is next?

Acting as the Incident Commander and determining your approach to the incident, your initial actions should include a **Size-Up**.

A size-up is done to develop initial incident objectives. Incident objectives will define what types of resources are required to respond to the incident. Finally, the resources the Incident Commander will manage affect which Command and General Staff positions will be activated to assist the IC in management of the incident.

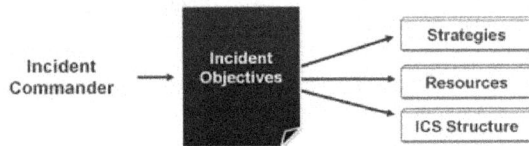

Visual 12:   So, what is next? (Continued)

The considerations for a size-up outlined in this course include:

1. Size-up the nature and magnitude of the incident.
2. Determine the hazards and safety concerns.
3. Determine Initial Priorities and immediate Resource Requirements.
4. Determine the location of the Incident Command Post and Staging Area.
5. Determine the Entrance and Exit Routes for Responders.

Again, you will need to first complete your size-up activities to determine the ICS sections that you will need to manage the incident.

We will walk through these initial actions that you will take as the first supervisor on scene.

Visual 13:　Size-Up the Nature and Magnitude

We will start size-up by looking at the first two considerations:

- Size-up the nature and magnitude of the incident
- Determine the hazards and safety concerns

Nature and magnitude refer to your assessment of what kind of incident you face. This can include the type of incident and the size and complexity of the event.

Visual 14:　Discussion Question

?

What is the nature of the incident on the previous screen?

Visual 15:   Incident Typing

Type 1

You should recall from this course that a useful way of characterizing incidents is by incident typing.

Incidents are categorized into 5 types based on complexity. Type 5 incidents are the least complex and Type 1 incidents are the most complex.

Factors that impact the determination of incident type include size of the ICS structure, number of resources employed, and the length of time the incident response is anticipated to last.

Complexity

Type 5

Visual 16:   Discussion Question

Review the following definitions of the Incident Type.

- TYPE 5 INCIDENT: One or two single response resources with up to 6 response personnel, Incident expected to last only a few hours, no ICS Command and General Staff positions activated.
- TYPE 4 INCIDENT: Several single response resources required, response will be limited to one operational period, select ICS Command and General Staff activated only as needed.
- TYPE 3 INCIDENT: Resource requirements will exceed the initial response resources, may extend into multiple operational periods, some or all ICS Command and General Staff are activated.
- TYPE 2 INCIDENT: Regional or National resources will be required, the incident will extend into multiple operational periods, most or all ICS Command and General Staff positions are filled.
- TYPE 1 INCIDENT: National level resources are required, the incident will extend into multiple operational periods, all ICS Command and General Staff positions are utilized, and Branches need to be established.

Incident Type

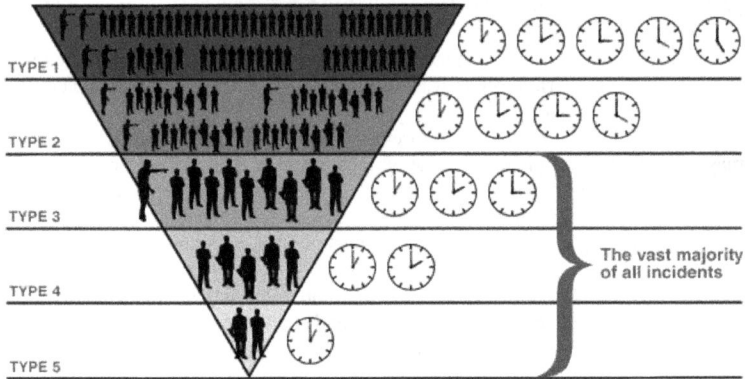

Clocks do not depict length of incident time.

Visual 17:   Discussion Question

?

What incident type is appropriate for the incident in this scenario?

Visual 18: Hazards and Safety Concerns

Understanding that this is a Type 4 Incident should already give you a framework to understand the number of resources you will need, how long the response may take, and the need to establish some ICS Command and General Staff for the incident.

The next part of the Initial Response Activities is to determine the hazards and safety concerns in the incident.

Thinking through the hazards and safety concerns is an important exercise for the Incident Commander or Unified Command. You must define the problems that you face before you can determine and prioritize the actions that you need to take in response to the incident.

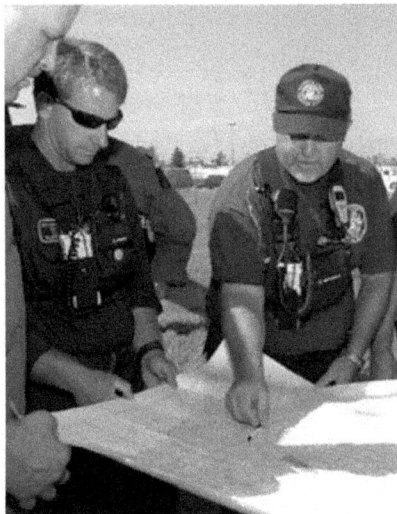

Visual 19:   Activity 8.2: Hazards and Safety Concerns

Activity Purpose: To practice identifying hazards and safety concerns.

Time: 10 minutes

Instructions: Working with your team . . .

1. Review the excerpt from the scenario below.
2. Identify the hazards and safety concerns.
3. Choose a spokesperson. Be prepared to present your answer to the class in 10 minutes.

Scenario:

Several people were injured as the large truck passed through the crowd and there may be deaths. There is disorder as some attempt to flee and others try to help. The tanker truck is an active fire that must be suppressed and could spread to nearby structures. The building and utilities (power, water, and gas) could be damaged and may present additional hazards to people in the affected area.

Activity 8.2: Hazards and Safety Concerns

Activity Purpose: To practice identifying hazards and safety concerns.

Time: 10 minutes

Instructions: Working with your team . . .

1. Review the excerpt from the scenario below.
2. Identify the hazards and safety concerns.
3. Choose a spokesperson. Be prepared to present your answer to the class in 10 minutes.

Instructor Note

Scenario:

Several people were injured as the large truck passed through the crowd and there may be deaths. There is disorder as some attempt to flee and others try to help. The tanker truck is an active fire that must be suppressed and could spread to nearby structures. The building and utilities (power, water, and gas) could be damaged and may present additional hazards to people in the affected area.

Visual 20:   Determine Initial Priorities & Immediate Resource Requirements

Now that you have defined the nature and magnitude of the incident and understand the hazards and safety concerns that you are faced with, you can start determining priorities and resources.

Let's start by reviewing two of the NIMS Management Characteristics that apply to determining priorities:

- **Management by Objectives:** Identify response priorities and objectives and define the resources required to achieve the objectives. This is a key activity that must be documented.
- **Incident Action Planning:** Incident objectives, tactics and assignments for operations and support are recorded and communicated through an Incident Action Plan (IAP). While this may not start as an extensive written document early in a response, as incidents increase in size, complexity, and length, it is increasingly important to document incident response activities.

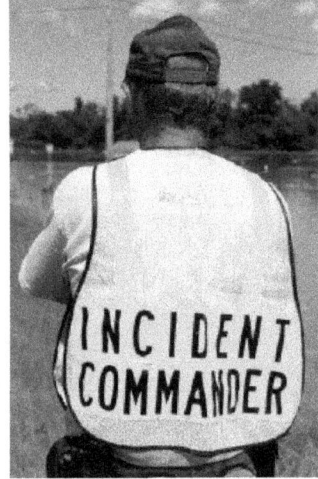

Visual 21:   Activity 8.3: Incident Objectives

Activity Purpose: To give the students practice at writing "SMART" incident objectives for various hazards and safety concerns.

Time: 15 minutes

Instructions: Working in your team:

1. Review the Hazards and Safety concerns on the chart in your Student Manual.
2. Using the chart included in your SM, determine what actions must be taken in response to the incident. Develop some simple objectives utilizing the "SMART" approach - incident objectives should be Specific, Measurable, Action-oriented, Realistic and Time-sensitive.
3. List the "SMART" incident objectives on chart paper.
4. Choose a spokesperson and be ready to present your objectives to the class in 15 minutes.

Activity 8.3 Incident Objectives

	Activity 8.3: Incident Objectives
	Activity Purpose: To give the students practice at writing "SMART" incident objectives for various hazards and safety concerns.
	Time: 15 minutes
	Instructions: Working in your team:
Activity	1. Review the Hazards and Safety concerns on the chart in your Student Manual.
	2. Using the chart, determine what actions must be taken in response to the incident. Develop some simple objectives utilizing the "SMART" approach - incident objectives should be Specific, Measurable, Action-oriented, Realistic and Time-sensitive.
	3. List the "SMART" incident objectives on chart paper.
	4. Choose a spokesperson and be ready to present your objectives to the class in 15 minutes.

Activity 8.3: Incident Objectives

Now you need to determine what actions must be taken in response to the incident.

Develop some simple objectives for a few of the previously identified incident hazards and safety concerns, and remember to utilize the "SMART" approach discussed in this course: incident objectives should be Specific, Measurable, Action-oriented, Realistic and Time-sensitive.

Hazards and Safety Concerns	Objectives
Untreated, immobile injured personnel	
Fire and flammable gasses	
Fleeing crowd and traffic congestion	

Visual 22:   Discussion Question

?

You have a lot of objectives for this incident. You will be pursuing multiple objectives simultaneously, but you also need to understand the priority of your objectives.

Take a look at the incident objectives you developed, which do you assess as your top priority objective?

Visual 23:   Determine Initial Priorities and Immediate Resource Requirements (Continued)

Once you have determined your objectives and priorities, you should next determine the resources that you will need to respond to the incident and accomplish your objectives.

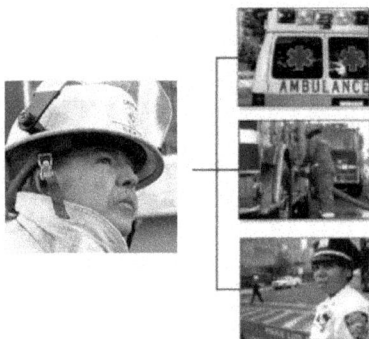

Visual 24: Activity 8.4: Defining Resources

Activity Purpose: To allow students practice defining resources for Incident Objectives.

Time: 10 minutes

Instructions: Working in your team:

1. Review the Incident Objectives you just created in the previous activity.
2. Using the list of resources provided below, identify which resources you would need to accomplish your incident objectives.
3. List the resources on chart paper.
4. Choose a spokesperson and be ready to present your resources to the class in 10 minutes.

Resources:

- Fire Trucks with Firefighter Personnel
- Ambulances with Medical Personnel
- Hazmat Team
- Law Enforcement Traffic Control
- Law Enforcement Investigators
- Fire Investigators
- Medical Examiner / Coroner

- Public Works - Electrical
- Public Works - Water
- Public Works - Gas
- Urban Search and Rescue Team
- Wildland Firefighting Teams
- K-9 Bomb Detection Dogs
- Explosive Ordnance Disposal Team

Activity 8.4: Defining Resources

Activity Purpose: To allow students practice defining resources for incident Objectives.

Time: 10 minutes

Instructions: Working in your team:

1. Review the Incident Objectives you just created in the previous activity.
2. Using the list of resources provided below, identify which resources you would need to accomplish your incident objectives.
3. List the resources on chart paper.
4. Choose a spokesperson and be ready to present your resources to the class in 10 minutes.

Activity

Resources:

- Fire Trucks with Firefighter Personnel
- Ambulances with Medical Personnel
- Hazmat Team
- Law Enforcement Traffic Control
- Law Enforcement Investigators
- Fire Investigators
- Medical Examiner / Coroner

- Public Works - Electrical
- Public Works - Water
- Public Works - Gas
- Urban Search and Rescue Team
- Wildland Firefighting Teams
- K-9 Bomb Detection Dogs
- Explosive Ordnance Disposal Team

Note

Remember the following NIMS Management Characteristics that can be applied to determining resource requirements:

- **Comprehensive Resource Management:** what resources are available for assignment or allocation (personnel, equipment, teams, and facilities)? IC/ UC can draw for pre-existing plans and resource management tools to assist in determining what resources are readily available and which must be filled externally.
- **Incident Facilities and Locations:** what facilities are required to manage the incident and where will they be located?
- **Integrated Communications:** can all disciplines and organizations involved in incident management and response communicate effectively. Are there any communication gaps that must be addressed?

Visual 25:   Determine Initial Priorities & Immediate Resource Requirements (Cont)

Before we move on from resources let's review a few more NIMS Management Characteristics that can be applied to managing resources:

- **Common Terminology:** Using standard terms for resources can help to ensure that when you request a resource it meets your requirements.
- **Accountability:** You will need processes to record and report the status of all incident resources from the time they arrive on the incident until they are returned to their jurisdiction.
- **Deployment:** You will need to control deployment of resources to ensure that you receive only what you have requested. Unrequested resources can take up space needed for requested resources and can create additional management requirements on the Incident Command or Unified Command.

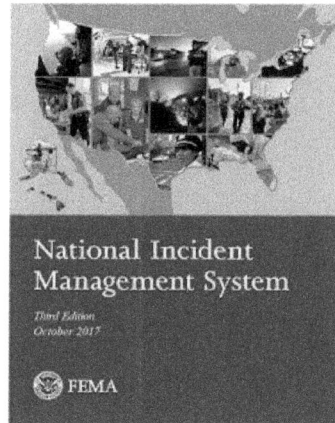

National Incident Management System

Third Edition
October 2017

FEMA

Visual 26:   Determine Incident Locations

Congratulations, you have completed the first
three initial response actions:

- Size-up the nature and magnitude of the
  incident
- Determine the hazards and safety concerns
- Determine initial priorities and immediate
  resource requirements

Next you have to consider a few issues associated
with site control:

- Determine the location of the Incident
  Command Post and staging area
- Determine the entrance and exit routes for
  responders

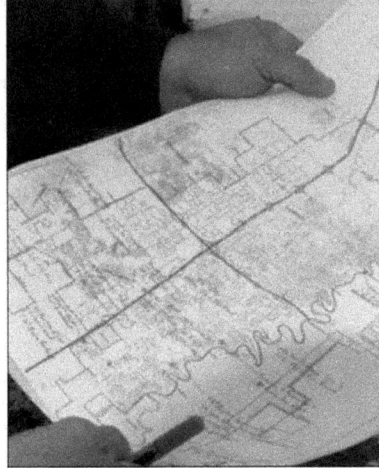

Visual 27:   Activity 8.5: Determining Incident Locations

Activity Purpose: To give students an opportunity to practice determining incident locations

Time: 10 minutes

Instructions: Working in your team:

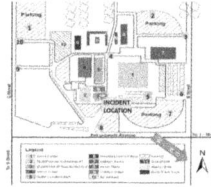

1. Review the map and indicate where you would place the following incident locations:

   - Incident Command Post
   - Staging Area
   - Entry point for responders
   - Exit point for responders

2. Choose a spokesperson and be ready to present your answers to the class in 10 minutes.

Activity 8.5: Determining Incident Locations

Activity Purpose: To give students an opportunity to practice determining incident locations

Time: 10 minutes

Instructions: Working in your team:

Activity

1. Review the map and indicate where you would place the following incident locations:

   - Incident Command Post
   - Staging Area
   - Entry point for responders
   - Exit point for responders

2. Choose a spokesperson and be ready to present your answers to the class in 10 minutes.

Activity 8.5: Determining Incident Locations - larger map

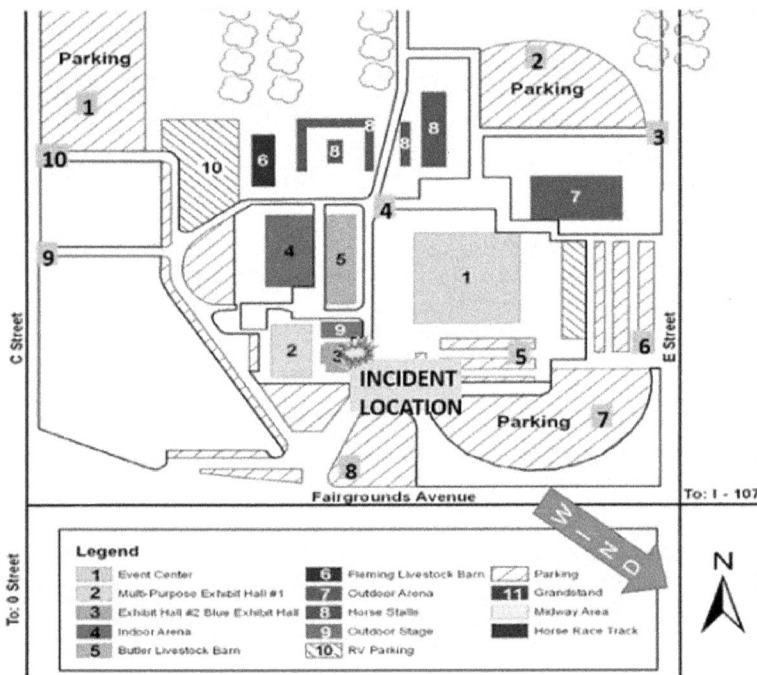

Visual 28:   Establish an ICS Structure

Acting as the Incident Commander you have completed a size-up to include identifying hazards and safety issues, setting priorities, determining resources, and defining key initial incident management locations.

Now that you understand what you are trying to accomplish and what resources you will be managing, you will need to define the ICS structure that will be needed to support management of the incident.

At this point in the scenario, the Incident Command likely consists of the Fire Chief working over the hood of a command vehicle. Additional resources will be arriving soon and the Incident Commander will need additional staff personnel to help in the management in the incident response.

	Establish an ICS Structure (Continued)
	There are several NIMS Management Characteristics that can be applied to determining the appropriate ICS structure for an incident:
Note	• **Chain of Command and Unity of Command:** All resources should work for a single general staff section and all general staff sections should report to and receive direction from a single IC. • **Manageable Span of Control:** the ICS structure must be of a sufficient size to assist the IC in effectively managing the incident. A key to this is constraining the number of subordinates or functions that each supervisor manages. • **Modular Organization:** what pieces of the ICS structure are needed to manage the incident? Think ahead to the next operational period because what you need then often must be asked for now.

Visual 29: Establish an ICS Structure (Cont)

What ICS Command and General Staff positions will you need to manage the incident?

Remember that the Incident Commander/Unified Command is responsible for performing all of these functions personally until he or she activates that function.

- Incident Command
- Public Information
- Safety
- Liaison
- Operations
- Planning
- Logistics
- Finance/Administration

Visual 30:   Establish an ICS Structure (Cont)

We previously assessed that this is a Type 4 Incident.

We expect several pieces of fire apparatus, ambulance crews, and law enforcement personnel to be involved. Between the incident site, the staging area, and the perimeter we can assume that at least 30 Law Enforcement, Fire, and EMS personnel will be involved in the incident response. These personnel will be distributed across at six to ten separate locations in and around the fairgrounds.

Visual 31:   Establish an ICS Structure (Cont)

For the purposes of this activity, we will only look at the eight Command Staff and General Staff positions.

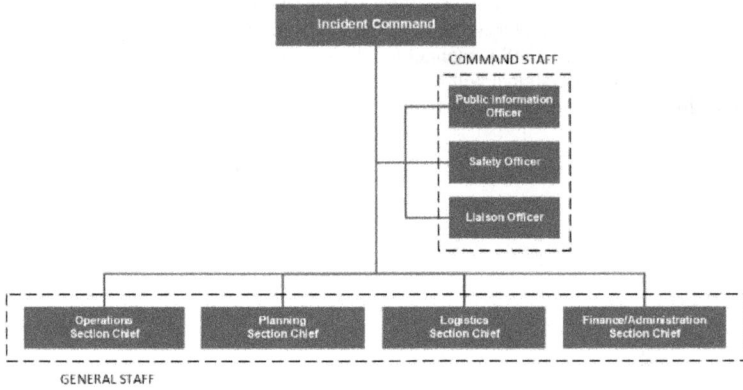

Visual 32:   Establish an ICS Structure (Cont)

Recall what function each Command and General Staff position performs:

- **Public Information Officer (PIO)** interfaces with the public, media, and others needing incident information.
- **Safety Officer** monitors incident operations and advises the Incident Command on matters relating to health and safety.
- **Liaison Officer** serves as the Incident Command's point of contact for organizations not included in the Unified Command.
- **Operations Section** plans and performs tactical activities to achieve the Incident Objectives established by the Incident Command.
- **Planning Section** personnel collect, evaluate, and disseminate incident information to the IC/UC and other incident personnel.
- **Logistics Section** personnel are responsible for providing services and support for the incident.
- IC/UC establishes a **Finance/Administration Section** when the incident management activities require on-scene or incident-specific finance and administrative support services.

Visual 33:   Activity 8.6: Staff Selection Practice

Activity Purpose: To allow students an opportunity to analyze the incident and select the appropriate staffing.

Time: 10 minutes

Instructions: Working in your team:

1. Review the scenario.
2. Determine the staff required to manage this incident.
3. Choose a spokesperson and be ready to present your answers to the class in 10 minutes.

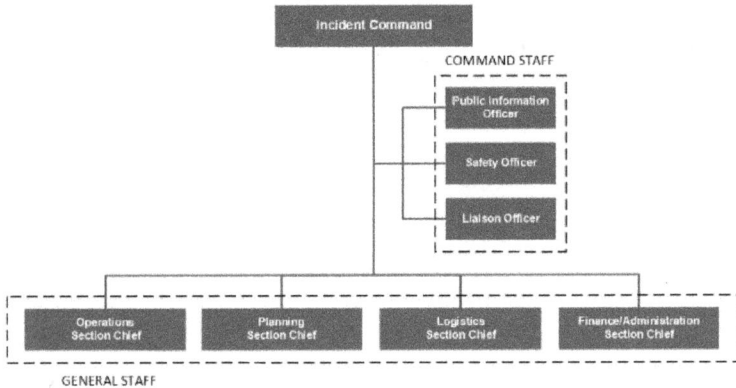

Activity 8.6: Staff Selection Practice

Activity Purpose: To allow students an opportunity to analyze the incident and select the appropriate staffing.

Time: 10 minutes

Instructions: Working in your team:

Activity

1. Review the scenario.
2. Determine the staff required to manage this incident.
3. Choose a spokesperson and be ready to present your answers to the class in 10 minutes.

Visual 34: Scenario Part 2

It is now just after 6 p.m. and the situation appears to be getting worse.

The initial assessment of several injuries was incorrect. There are over a dozen injuries and at least three dead.

The vehicle fire spread quickly to the building, igniting a damaged natural gas line in a kitchen area. The combination of explosion, fire, and collision damage caused the building to partially collapse. The fire continues to burn and now threatens other surrounding structures.

The crowds are under control, but traffic has not yet completely cleared from the area and continues to slow the ingress and egress of emergency management resources.

The vehicle driver has not been found and the origin and contents of the large truck have not been identified. This raises new concerns that this could have been an intentional act and that the truck could have been transporting something hazardous.

This incident has increased in size and complexity and will extend into at least one more operational period.

Visual 35:   Activity 8.7: Expanding Incident

Activity Purpose: To apply key concepts to analyze incidents.

Time: 10 minutes

Instructions: Working with your team . . .

1. Based on the scenario update, review the factors that your instructor has assigned to you.
2. Develop answers for each assigned factor.
3. Choose a spokesperson. Be prepared to present your answers to the class in 10 minutes.

Activity 8.7: Expanding Incident

Activity Purpose: To apply key concepts to analyze incidents.

Time: 10 minutes

Instructions: Working with your team . . .

Activity

1. Based on the scenario update, review the factors that your instructor has assigned to you.
2. Develop answers for each assigned factor.
3. Choose a spokesperson. Be prepared to present your answers to the class in 10 minutes.

Visual 36:   Transfer of Command (Continued)

The initial Incident Commander may continue to serve as a member of a Unified Command. It is also possible that the increase in complexity will lead to the appointment of more senior personnel to Incident Command.

Remember that **Establishment and Transfer of Command** is a NIMS Management Characteristic. You must clearly state and record when command is transferred.

The Transfer of Command should be conducted to create minimal disruption to the incident. Whenever possible, the Transfer of Command should include a complete briefing on the situation conducted face to face with the new Incident Commander or Unified Command.

The NIMS Management Characteristic **Incident Action Planning** also applies here. Incident objectives, tactics, and assignments for operations and support should be recorded and communicated through an Incident Action Plan (IAP). As your incident increased in size, complexity, and length, you should have started to document incident response activities in a written plan.

The ICS Form 201 is a standard format to record key situational information and document actions taken on an incident.

Visual 37:   Lesson Summary

You have completed the Application Activity. You have applied these key concepts to a scenario-based activity:

- NIMS Management Characteristics
- Incident Command and Unified Command
- Initial Size-up
- Developing Incident Objectives
- Determining Resource Requirements
- Determining Appropriate ICS Structure for an Incident
- Transfer of Command

Lesson 9: Course Summary

Visual 1:   Lesson 9 Overview

This lesson provides a brief summary of the Basic Incident Command System for Initial Response course content. After reviewing the summary information, you will receive instructions for taking the course Final Exam.

Visual 2: Lesson 1: Course Overview (NIMS & ICS Review)

- NIMS provides the Nation with a standardized framework for incident management.
- ICS, a part of NIMS, is a management system used to meet the demands of incidents large or small, planned or unplanned.

The NIMS Management Characteristics:

- Common Terminology
- Modular Organization
- Management by Objectives
- Incident Action Planning
- Manageable Span of Control
- Incident Facilities and Locations
- Comprehensive Resource Management

- Integrated Communications
- Establishment and Transfer of Command
- Unified Command
- Chain of Command and Unity of Command
- Accountability
- Dispatch/Deployment
- Information and Intelligence Management

Visual 3:   Lesson 2: Incident Command and Unified Command

- Chain of Command is the line of authority that flows down through the organizational structure.

- Unity of Command means that each individual will be assigned and report to only one supervisor.

- Unity of Command is different from Unified Command; Unified Command is established when no one jurisdiction, agency, or organization has primary authority, therefore there is no one clear Incident Commander. These multiple agencies work together to communicate and make command decisions.

- Communication during an incident may be formal or informal

  - Formal communications must be used for work assignments, resource requests, and progress reports.
  - Informal communication is used to exchange incident or event information only.

Visual 4:   Lesson 2: Incident Command and Unified Command

- All levels of leadership on an incident should understand and practice the leadership principles, have a commitment to duty, and take actions that prioritize the safety of personnel.

- Clear communication is the responsibility of all responders in order to accomplish incident objectives. Incident Management Assessments may be conducted by leadership after an incident to help personnel process what happened and why.

- ICS utilizes a Modular Organization so that the organization can expand and contract as an incident grows and shrinks. This modular organization helps maintain an effective span of control.

- Manageable span of control with Modular Organization is accomplished by organizing resources into Teams, Divisions, Groups, Branches, or Sections. Leadership in each organizational level holds a unique title.

- The flexibility allowed for in ICS does is not override the importance of Common Terminology. Common Terminology must be used to maintain clear communication, whether formal or informal.

Visual 5:   Lesson 3: Delegation of Authority and Management by Objectives

- Authority is the right or obligation to act on behalf of a department, agency, or jurisdiction.

- The scope of authority that an Incident Commander has is determined by existing laws, policies, and procedures. Additional authority may be delegated when necessary.

- Delegation of authority is the process of granting authority to an individual or agency to carry out specific functions during an incident.

- Delegation of authority does NOT relieve the granting entity of the responsibility for that function. Authority can be delegated; responsibility cannot.

Visual 6:   Lesson 3: Delegation of Authority and Management by Objectives

- When needed, a delegation of authority should contain elements related to restrictions, external implications and considerations, and planning and communication processes.

- Authority is implemented by the Incident Commander through the management of objectives. Effective Incident Objectives should be SMART. Objectives are not tactics or strategies; they state what needs to be accomplished, not how to do it.

- Objectives are a part of the Incident Action Plan, which is completed each operational period and outlines incident-specific information. It is created through a process known as the Operational Period Planning Cycle (Planning P).

- Incident Command, as well as Command and General Staff, should also have a working knowledge of other preparedness plans, such as EOPs, SOGs, SOPs, and mutual aid agreements.

Visual 7:   Lesson 4: Functional Areas and Positions

- The Incident Commander oversees the incident, sets incident objectives, and approves the IAP.

- Command Staff include the Public Information Officer, Safety Officer, and Liaison Officer.

- The Incident Commander also oversees four sections of the ICS organizational structure: Operations, Planning, Logistics, and Finance & Administration. Each of these sections is responsible for a different function during an incident; Sections are led by the General Staff who report to the Incident Commander. General Staff are titled as Section Chiefs.

- Operations directs and coordinates all incident tactical operations.

Visual 8:   Lesson 4: Functional Areas and Positions

- Planning maintains resource and situation status, prepares the IAP and other documents, and looks beyond the current operational period to anticipate potential future problems or events.

- Logistics is responsible for all support requirements, including communications, facility supplies, medical needs, and food and drink for incident personnel.

- Finance/Administration provides administrative and financial support services. This includes handling claims related to property damage, injuries, and fatalities.

- ICS Forms help communicate and organize information between Command, Command Staff, General Staff, and other incident personnel.

Visual 9:   Lesson 5: Incident Briefings and Meetings

- Different meetings and briefings are used during the Incident Action Planning Process to share information.

- Briefings should be concise and may occur at the staff, field, or section level.

- Information shared during a briefing includes the current situation and objectives, safety issues and emergency procedures, work tasks, facilities and work areas, communication protocols, expectations, resource acquisition procedures, work schedules, and questions or concerns.

- The Operational Period Briefing is led by the Incident Commander to present the IAP. Command and General Staff will also participate to share important information.

Visual 10:   Lesson 6: Organizational Flexibility

- NIMS requires organizational standardization use of Common Terminology; however, ICS is still flexible due to its Modular Organization.
- Functions and positions within the organizational structure are activated and filled based on the needs and demand of an incident. The ICS organizational structure will expand and contract with the incident.
- Personnel may hold multiple titles within an incident's organizational structure, but the titles must keep consistent with NIMS titles. Titles may not be shortened or combined.
- Proper Resource Management is essential to maintaining an accurate and up-to-date picture of resource utilization and needs.
- Incidents are typed based on size and complexity. Incident types move from Type 5 as the least complex to Type 1 as the most complex.

Visual 11:   Lesson 7: Transfer of Command

- Transfer of Command is the process of moving the responsibility for incident command from one Incident Commander to another Incident Commander or Unified Command.

- Transfer of Command should take place face-to-face when possible and include a complete briefing that captures essential information.

- The transfer of command briefing should include elements such as the situation status, incident objectives and priorities, current organization, resource information, incident communications plan, etc.

- A notification of the time and date that the transfer of command becomes effective should be communicated to all incident personnel.

Visual 12:   Congratulations!

You should now be able to demonstrate knowledge of how to manage an initial response to an incident.

The course specifically discussed:

- Incident Command and Unified Command
- Delegation of Authority & Management by Objectives
- Functional Areas & Positions
- Incident Briefings and Meetings
- Organizational Flexibility
- Transfer of Command
- Application of ICS for Initial Response

Visual 13:   IS-200.c Final Exam Instructions

When the review is completed, follow these Final Exam instructions:

1. Take a few moments to review your Student Manual and identify any questions.
2. Make sure that you get all of your questions answered prior to beginning the final test.
3. When taking the test online …

   - Go to http://training.fema.gov/IS/crslist.asp and click on the link for IS-0200.c.
   - Click on "Take Final Exam."
   - Read each item carefully.
   - Check your work before submitting your answers.

Visual 14:   Certificate of Completion

To receive a certificate of completion, you must take the multiple-choice Final Exam and score at least 75 percent on the test.

Upon successful completion of the Final Exam, you will receive an e-mail message with a link to your electronic certification.

Visual 15:   Course Evaluation

Completing the course evaluation form is important. Your comments will be used to evaluate the effectiveness of this course and make changes for future versions.

Please use the course evaluation forms provided by the organization sponsoring the course.